DISCARD

Global Resources

Opposing Viewpoints®

OTHER BOOKS OF RELATED INTEREST

OPPOSING VIEWPOINTS SERIES

Africa
America Beyond 2001
Animal Rights
Biomedical Ethics
Endangered Species
The Environment
Genetic Engineering
Global Warming
Population
The Third World
21st Century Earth
Water

CURRENT CONTROVERSIES SERIES

Energy Alternatives
Garbage and Waste
Hunger
Native American Rights
Pollution

AT ISSUE SERIES

Rainforests

Global Resources

Opposing Viewpoints®

David L. Bender, *Publisher*
Bruno Leone, *Executive Editor*
Brenda Stalcup, *Managing Editor*
Scott Barbour, *Senior Editor*
Charles P. Cozic, *Book Editor*

OPPOSING
VIEWPOINTS®
SERIES

Greenhaven Press, Inc., San Diego, California

Cover photo: Brent Peterson

Library of Congress Cataloging-in-Publication Data

Global resources : opposing viewpoints / Charles P. Cozic, book editor.
    p.   cm. — (Opposing viewpoints series)
    Includes bibliographical references and index.
    ISBN 1-56510-673-3 (lib. bdg. : alk. paper). —
ISBN 1-56510-672-5 (pbk. : alk. paper)
    1. Economic development—Environmental aspects. 2. Natural
resources—Management. 3. Conservation of natural resources.
I. Cozic, Charles P., 1957– . II. Series: Opposing viewpoints series
(Unnumbered)
HQ75.6.G56 1998
333.7—dc21   97-19698
                                                                              CIP

Greenhaven Press, Inc., P.O. Box 289009
San Diego, CA 92198-9009

"CONGRESS SHALL MAKE NO LAW... ABRIDGING THE FREEDOM OF SPEECH, OR OF THE PRESS."

First Amendment to the U.S. Constitution

The basic foundation of our democracy is the First Amendment guarantee of freedom of expression. The Opposing Viewpoints Series is dedicated to the concept of this basic freedom and the idea that it is more important to practice it than to enshrine it.

CONTENTS

WHY CONSIDER OPPOSING VIEWPOINTS?

"The only way in which a human being can make some approach to knowing the whole of a subject is by hearing what can be said about it by persons of every variety of opinion and studying all modes in which it can be looked at by every character of mind. No wise man ever acquired his wisdom in any mode but this."

John Stuart Mill

In our media-intensive culture it is not difficult to find differing opinions. Thousands of newspapers and magazines and dozens of radio and television talk shows resound with differing points of view. The difficulty lies in deciding which opinion to agree with and which "experts" seem the most credible. The more inundated we become with differing opinions and claims, the more essential it is to hone critical reading and thinking skills to evaluate these ideas. Opposing Viewpoints books address this problem directly by presenting stimulating debates that can be used to enhance and teach these skills. The varied opinions contained in each book examine many different aspects of a single issue. While examining these conveniently edited opposing views, readers can develop critical thinking skills such as the ability to compare and contrast authors' credibility, facts, argumentation styles, use of persuasive techniques, and other stylistic tools. In short, the Opposing Viewpoints Series is an ideal way to attain the higher-level thinking and reading skills so essential in a culture of diverse and contradictory opinions.

In addition to providing a tool for critical thinking, Opposing Viewpoints books challenge readers to question their own strongly held opinions and assumptions. Most people form their opinions on the basis of upbringing, peer pressure, and personal, cultural, or professional bias. By reading carefully balanced opposing views, readers must directly confront new ideas as well as the opinions of those with whom they disagree. This is not to simplistically argue that everyone who reads opposing views will—or should—change his or her opinion. Instead, the series enhances readers' understanding of their own views by encouraging confrontation with opposing ideas. Careful examination of others' views can lead to the readers' understanding of the logical inconsistencies in their own opinions, perspective on why they hold an opinion, and the consideration of the possibility that their opinion requires further evaluation.

Evaluating Other Opinions

To ensure that this type of examination occurs, Opposing Viewpoints books present all types of opinions. Prominent spokespeople on different sides of each issue as well as well-known professionals from many disciplines challenge the reader. An additional goal of the series is to provide a forum for other, less known, or even unpopular viewpoints. The opinion of an ordinary person who has had to make the decision to cut off life support from a terminally ill relative, for example, may be just as valuable and provide just as much insight as a medical ethicist's professional opinion. The editors have two additional purposes in including these less known views. One, the editors encourage readers to respect others' opinions—even when not enhanced by professional credibility. It is only by reading or listening to and objectively evaluating others' ideas that one can determine whether they are worthy of consideration. Two, the inclusion of such viewpoints encourages the important critical thinking skill of objectively evaluating an author's credentials and bias. This evaluation will illuminate an author's reasons for taking a particular stance on an issue and will aid in readers' evaluation of the author's ideas.

As series editors of the Opposing Viewpoints Series, it is our hope that these books will give readers a deeper understanding of the issues debated and an appreciation of the complexity of even seemingly simple issues when good and honest people disagree. This awareness is particularly important in a democratic society such as ours in which people enter into public debate to determine the common good. Those with whom one disagrees should not be regarded as enemies but rather as people whose views deserve careful examination and may shed light on one's own.

Thomas Jefferson once said that "difference of opinion leads to inquiry, and inquiry to truth." Jefferson, a broadly educated man, argued that "if a nation expects to be ignorant and free . . . it expects what never was and never will be." As individuals and as a nation, it is imperative that we consider the opinions of others and examine them with skill and discernment. The Opposing Viewpoints Series is intended to help readers achieve this goal.

David L. Bender & Bruno Leone,
Series Editors

Greenhaven Press anthologies primarily consist of previously published material taken from a variety of sources, including periodicals, books, scholarly journals, newspapers, government documents, and position papers from private and public organizations. These original sources are often edited for length and to ensure their accessibility for a young adult audience. The anthology editors also change the original titles of these works in order to clearly present the main thesis of each viewpoint and to explicitly indicate the opinion presented in the viewpoint. These alterations are made in consideration of both the reading and comprehension levels of a young adult audience. Every effort is made to ensure that Greenhaven Press accurately reflects the original intent of the authors included in this anthology.

INTRODUCTION

"Natural resources are being depleted most rapidly in those countries where populations are growing in leaps and bounds."

—Paul Kennedy

"To our knowledge, the world has never run out of a non-renewable resource, and there are no signs that it is doing so now."

—Jane S. Shaw and Richard L. Stroup

In his famous text *An Essay on the Principle of Population* (1798), English clergyman Thomas Malthus argued that the human population tends to increase more rapidly than food supplies and that population growth would ultimately lead to disease, starvation, and war. Malthus's argument remained popular for decades, and his ominous forecasts are currently mirrored in various predictions that the human population will be unable to sustain itself in the future.

Many researchers and scientists calculate that because the world's population could double to more than ten billion as early as the year 2050, increased human consumption and activity will rapidly deplete or exhaust the earth's vital natural resources. Others disagree, arguing that human activity is not critically reducing supplies of global resources. They contend that due to frequent discoveries of new reserves, known supplies of many resources are in fact increasing.

Some researchers blame industrial societies, particularly the United States, for extensive resource depletion. Dartmouth College environmental studies professor Donella Meadows states, "If everyone on Earth lived like the average North American and we utilized fully every productive acre (leaving no wilderness), we would need three Earths to support the present world population." According to these experts, humanity's growing impact on land and natural resources is straining the world's ability to support its increasing population. University of British Columbia planning professor William Rees calls this effect the "ecological footprint."

Many observers warn that humanity's ecological footprint is growing at a dangerous pace. Stanford University professor of population Paul R. Ehrlich and his wife, Stanford biologist Anne H. Ehrlich, maintain that the "explosion of human numbers has been combined with a four-fold increase in consumption per person. The result is a twenty-fold escalation since 1850 of the pressure humanity places on its environment." The Ehrlichs are among those who contend that population increases will exert more pressure on land, soils, forests, water, and other resources. As Princeton University sociologist and demographer Charles F. Westoff writes, "Growing populations multiply whatever environmentally destructive behavior is present."

Beginning in 1970, Meadows and others at the Massachusetts Institute of Technology administered a computer simulation model called World3 that studied such variables as population, pollution, and the use of energy and other resources. In their 1972 book *The Limits to Growth*, these researchers cautioned that humanity was fast approaching the limits—especially the environmental limits—to the rapid growth of civilization and its consumption of global resources. They maintained that if increases in population, industrialization, and resource depletion continued unabated, limits to growth would be reached early in the twenty-first century, causing drastic declines in energy use as well as food and industrial production. The preface to their 1992 update, *Beyond the Limits to Growth*, notes that "the world has already overshot some of its limits, and if present trends remain unchanged, we face the virtually certain prospect of a global economic collapse."

However, other observers disagree with these predictions. They argue that although human consumption of global resources has increased, the supply of resources is not in jeopardy and remains abundant. These experts note that because of technological advances, more supplies of global resources are being discovered or conserved. Some maintain, for example, that raw materials such as lead, tin, wood, and zinc, which are used in manufacturing, are being conserved due to the increased use of other materials, including aluminum, glass, plastic, and rubber. Also, new mining methods use bacteria, electricity, and foaming agents to recover copper, gold, and other minerals from low-grade ores that would otherwise be discarded. Economist Julian L. Simon asserts that the prices of most resources are decreasing, suggesting that they are in ample supply. In Simon's words, "The real prices of food and of every other raw material are lower now than in earlier decades and centuries, indicating a trend of increased natural-resource availability rather than increased scarcity."

Simon and others also contend that since the known supplies of many global resources are increasing, humanity will not be hindered by limits to growth. As Cato Institute economist Stephen Moore writes, "The introduction of new technologies and innovations, which make us more efficient in consuming and producing natural resources, has meant that the earth's resources have continually become less of a limit to growth over time rather than more so." The downward trend in resource prices, Moore and others maintain, proves that resources are abundant and disproves the findings of the World3 model, which they claim did not use accurate data as input. Simon points out that the Club of Rome, an organization that sponsored the World3 model, later disavowed the Limits to Growth report for exaggerating the extent of resource depletion.

Furthermore, according to Eco-Scam author Ronald Bailey and researchers Michael Sanera and Jane S. Shaw, the dire predictions of The Limits to Growth have not come true since the book's publication. Sanera and Shaw write, "Oil is plentiful and cheap. The world did not run out of gold by 1981, or zinc by 1990, or petroleum by 1992, as the book predicted." Bailey adds, "America's population has risen 22% and its economy has grown by more than 58%." He notes that "humanity hasn't come close to running out of any mineral resource." Even if some resources do become more scarce over time, Sanera and Shaw assert, price increases will cause producers to seek cheaper substitute materials, thus maintaining consumers' access to products and services. In their words, "The resources that we use will change over time. Materials that were previously unknown or neglected will provide the services we want."

The debate over the effects of population growth on the availability of global resources is a main theme in Global Resources: Opposing Viewpoints, which poses arguments on resource scarcity in the following chapters: Are Global Resources Being Depleted? What Agricultural Policies Should Be Pursued? What Energy Sources Should Be Pursued? How Can Global Resources Be Protected? The contributors in this anthology examine the availability of and dependence on the world's vital natural resources.

CHAPTER 1

ARE GLOBAL RESOURCES BEING DEPLETED?

Chapter Preface

More than one billion people depend on oil for transportation and various products and services, and oil provides nearly one-third of the world's energy supply. Many researchers contend that crude oil production will peak early in the twenty-first century and will subsequently decline, leading to inevitable oil shortages. Others disagree and assert that ample supplies make oil an abundant resource.

Regardless of whether oil production peaks in the early twenty-first century, many experts argue that there are enough oil reserves available to satisfy global demand for many decades. For example, the American Petroleum Institute (API) notes that an estimated 1.4 trillion to 2.1 trillion barrels of oil worldwide are available for production. At the current rate of consumption, the API maintains, this is enough oil to last between sixty-three and ninety-five years. Moreover, according to the API, "If economically feasible ways to extract and refine unconventional sources of oil are found, our oil supply could be extended for hundreds of years."

But many environmental activists and others warn that because the largest oil fields have already been discovered and because oil production will soon decline, the world should prepare now for a forthcoming oil shortage and potential crisis. According to petroleum consultant and geologist Colin Campbell, "By now, the whole world has been thoroughly explored. It has become clear that no new provinces comparable with the North Sea and Alaska await discovery." In the words of Christopher Flavin and Nicholas Lenssen, authors of *Power Surge*, "The world oil market is entering a danger period" due to the likelihood of higher oil prices and greater dependence on the oil-rich Middle East, which "is likely to remain dangerously unstable."

Oil is one of the world's most vital resources. In the following chapter, the authors debate whether this and other important global resources are being depleted.

"*A permanent oil shock is inevitable early in the twenty-first century.*"

GLOBAL OIL RESERVES ARE BEING EXHAUSTED

L.F. Ivanhoe

L.F. Ivanhoe is an energy exploration consultant in Ojai, California. In the following viewpoint, Ivanhoe asserts that high energy demands will soon exceed the production of crude oil from known reserves. Ivanhoe contends that because of the unlikelihood of discovering large oil fields, oil reserves will become rapidly depleted, thus producing a permanent oil shortage. According to Ivanhoe, this inevitable shortage will result in higher fuel prices, high inflation, and fuel rationing.

As you read, consider the following questions:

1. According to Ivanhoe, what was the peak year of oil discovery?
2. What is the difference between oil reserves and oil resources, according to Ivanhoe?
3. What does the author mean by "fruit salad" numbers?

From L.F. Ivanhoe, "Get Ready for Another Oil Shock." This article originally appeared in the January/February 1997 issue of the *Futurist* and is used with permission from the World Futurist Society, 7910 Woodmont Ave., Suite 450, Bethesda, MD 20814. 301/656-8274; fax 301/951-0394; e-mail wfsinfo@wfs.org.

A fter the oil crises of the 1970s, petroleum shortages disappeared and prices stabilized. The world stopped worrying about oil, but the grim fact remains that the world's petroleum reserves are limited, and they are rapidly being used up.

What happened in the 1970s was simply that prices rose suddenly, so the search for additional petroleum supplies became compelling and the incentives to conserve oil increased sharply. Shifts in supply and demand of all fuels solved the global petroleum problem.

But a much more serious problem looms in the future. Most of the world's large, economically viable oil fields have already been found, so a permanent oil shock is inevitable early in the twenty-first century. More Europeans than Americans are aware of this.

The question is not whether, but when, world crude oil productivity will start to decline, ushering in the permanent oil shock era. Some believe we have enough to last another 50 years at present rates. I disagree: Most of the large exploration targets for oil supply have been found, at the same time that the world's population (and, along with it, demand for energy) is exploding.

MODERN PETROLEUM TECHNOLOGY

Petroleum exploration is an efficient technical procedure. Shooting a modern seismic net of lines across any geologic/sedimentary basin will reveal virtually all significant prospects, thus showing oil companies where to lease for further test drilling. However, it is a fact that the largest oil and gas fields in any sedimentary basin or oil province are also the biggest targets and the easiest to find with any given technology; thus, they are normally found early in any exploration phase.

Today, there are virtually no areas where petroleum exploration cannot be successfully carried out if regional geological studies indicate a good chance of finding major petroleum fields (i.e., those with an ultimate recovery of more than 100 million barrels of oil).

The latest phase of petroleum exploration began with the introduction of 3-D digital seismic methods in the late 1970s. This technical refinement coincided with the Iran-Iraq War and the accompanying 1980 oil price surge to $40/barrel, which produced a global public energy panic. A worldwide exploration boom followed immediately to find oil anywhere outside the Persian Gulf.

Unfortunately, despite intense efforts by all of the world's oil companies, only a few of the new major fields promised by their geologists were actually found. The world's accessible oil provinces had all been previously recognized and most of their major fields found earlier. Numerous major finds had been made in the late 1960s, which brought on production offshore by new marine technologies during the mid-1970s in time to bring the OPEC [Organization of Petroleum Exporting Countries] producers to heel. No new major oil provinces (those producing 7 to 25 billion barrels) have been found since 1980.

FINITE RESERVES

The world is finite. The 1,311 known major and giant oil fields contain 94% of the world's known oil and are accordingly the most critical for future global oil supplies. . . . The peak global oil finding year was 1962. Since then, the global discovery rate has dropped sharply in all regions.

Modern three-dimensional seismic and horizontal-drilling techniques improved current oil recovery in known fields, but made no substantial change in global reserves or discoveries of major fields. When the world oil price collapsed in 1986, exploration funds and efforts were cut back drastically everywhere; and by 1989, all major companies were downsizing and eliminating most of their geological and geophysical staffs. The minimum six-year period needed to discover the five largest fields in any basin had passed without making enough discoveries to whet top management's enthusiasm, so the money dried up for all but prime prospects.

This is unfortunate, because the huge remaining resources postulated by scientists and reported in the *Oil and Gas Journal* and U.S. Geological Survey [USGS] publications will never be converted to reserves unless explored for. It is unlikely that increasing the global oil price to the 1980 maximum ($40/barrel) would make any substantial improvement in the discovery rate of new major fields, as the golden age of oil exploration passed its peak in 1962. For example, much of the current attraction for Russian oil deals is aimed at increasing production rather than exploring for new sources. Western petroleum engineers and service/supply companies are being used to get additional production out of known pools.

RESERVES VS. RESOURCES

There is a great deal of disagreement on the issue of future oil supply; one reason is that there is confusion among the terms used, such as active and inactive reserves, known and unknown resources, etc. Like the mining term *ore*, oil reserves are by definition economic or profitable. Oil resources, conversely, are less tangible. Two useful oil business terms are:

• *Reserves*—engineers' (conservative) opinions of how much oil is known to be producible, within a known time, with known techniques, at known costs, and in known fields. Conservative bankers will loan money on *reserves*.

• *Resources*—geologists' (optimistic) opinions of all undiscovered oil theoretically present in an area. Conservative bankers will NOT loan money on *resources*.

Petroleum explorers must find—and then petroleum engineers convert—theoretical resources into producible reserves. An example of a resource that will probably never become a reserve is gold dissolved in seawater.

Use of either term depends greatly on whose money is involved. "Resources" means using *your* money; "reserves" means using *my* money. Differences can be enormous. Government agencies and academic scientists tend to estimate resources, whereas industrial/oil companies appraise only reserves. The public, using its own money to buy gasoline, is interested in producible reserves, not in theoretical resources.

"Assessing world oil is only the beginning of the search for oil," says C.D. Masters, retired chief of U.S. Geological Survey Petroleum Resource Analysis. "Assessment means nothing more than a judgment on its occurrence. Whether it will be discovered depends on discovery activity." Well-intentioned but irresponsible scientists who continue to discuss resources rather than reserves may be a significant reason for the lack of realistic energy policies.

ACTIVE VS. INACTIVE RESERVES

Two more terms that cloud the oil-supply discussion are:

• *Active reserves*—those producible within the foreseeable future (i.e., 20 years or less); and

• *Inactive reserves*—those known to exist but not considered producible within 20 years; i.e., inaccessible or producible only with not-as-yet commercial methods, such as enhanced oil recovery. Conservative bankers will NOT loan money on inactive reserves.

Oil companies are in business to make money—not to find oil per se. What is the present economic value of oil to be produced more than 20 years in the future? Virtually zero, regardless of its price.

Scientific geological committees have recently blurred the discussion of known reserves by including inactive with active, thus artificially increasing the U.S. national reserves by redefining critical terms and using creative bookkeeping. Meanwhile, mature oil fields continue to decline, as predicted by engineers.

POLITICAL RESERVES

All government petroleum ministries have an inherent interest in announcing the "good news" of large national hydrocarbon reserves, inasmuch as large reserves are useful for national political prestige and in negotiations for OPEC production quotas, World Bank loans and grants, etc. Sudden unsubstantiated reserve increases announced by any government ministry should be viewed with considerable skepticism. They may be mostly the puffery of "political reserves" that will increase a nation's paper reserves but have no effect on ultimate oil production.

For instance, units of natural gas are commonly converted to barrels of oil equivalent (BOE) to increase a company's or nation's BOE reserves. However, natural gas is neither the economic nor the social equivalent of crude oil: It's not as convenient, safe, or flexible as oil.

Political reserves tend to lull the public, politicians, and stockbrokers into complacency. But the critical numbers are U.S. and world oil production and new oil field discoveries in recent years, and these numbers are not encouraging.

A major problem is that planners base their forecasts on what amounts to political reserves—numbers that are fudged (accidentally or intentionally) by the oil ministries responsible for providing statistics to international bodies. For example, the much-quoted annual BP [British Petroleum] Statistical Review of World Energy's tables and graphs on "Distribution of Oil Reserves in 1994" contains a fine-print footnote: "Estimates contained in this table are those published by the *Oil and Gas Journal* in its issue of December 26, 1994, plus an estimate of natural gas liquids for North America."

PROBLEMS WITH NUMBERS

One must go back to the *Oil and Gas Journal* (O&GJ) year-end reports to check each of the oil-producing nations' oil and gas reserves and production. On close examination, one soon runs into problems with the numbers. O&GJ merely compiles the *reserve* information provided annually by each country's government source. There is no way to check on the accuracy of foreign reports. To many foreign ministries, the O&GJ's requests for reserve data is either a sensitive state secret or a nuisance chore no one is critically concerned about. Due to ignorance or lack of guidance, a common answer is "same as last year." More than half of the 94 nations listed in O&GJ's 1994 report have the identical oil reserve numbers as a year earlier.

Some nations' numbers are obviously gross approximations. Iraq doubled its reported reserves from 47 Bbo [billion barrels of oil] to 100 Bbo in 1987—the number that Iraq still listed for its reserves eight years later. Who could prove Iraq wrong? And what difference would it make to Iraq if the world's economists and planners were misled by Saddam Hussein's petroleum ministry?

Even more egregious than the exaggerations of political reserves is the economists' treatment of the U.S. Geological Survey's *resource* numbers. These are commonly added to the O&GJ *reserves* to produce a grand total of each nation's "oil endowment." The sum of the two (unknown) values gives huge "fruit salad" numbers that are routinely and incorrectly called *reserves*. No time limits are set for discovering the USGS resources.

SHOCKS AND AFTERSHOCKS

By the year 2000, global population will be 50% greater than in 1975, with a corresponding increase in demand for crude oil. The industrializing countries (China, India, etc.) will soon become hard competitors with Western nations for world crude exports.

It is reluctantly concluded from the USGS's global discovery statistics that the world's total oil production might peak about the year 2010, after which the normal decline of the world's oil fields will take over. By 2050, oil production will be a small fraction of today's bounty.

The critical date is when global public demand will substantially exceed the available supply from the few Persian Gulf Moslem oil exporters. The permanent global oil shortage will begin when the world's oil demand exceeds global production—i.e., about 2010 if normal oil-fields decline occurs, or as early as 2000 if the world's key oil producer, Saudi Arabia, has serious political problems that curtail its exports. World oil production will thereafter continue to decline at a dwindling rate. (See Figure 1.)

This foreseeable energy/oil crisis will affect everyone. Governments will have the highest priorities for transportation fuels during an emergency. A sudden global crude oil shortage of 5% could bring back the gasoline lines of the 1970s—to the American public's surprise and dismay. But this time the oil shortage will be permanent.

Thus the question is not *whether* but *when* the foreseeable permanent oil crunch will occur. This next paralyzing and permanent oil shock will not be solved by any redistribution patterns or by economic cleverness, because it will be a consequence of pending and inexorable depletion of the world's conventional crude oil supply. Few economists can bring themselves to accept that the global oil supply is geologically finite.

FIGURE 1. WORLD OIL SUPPLY

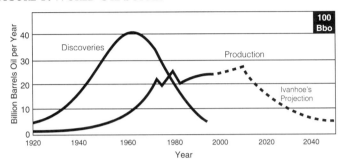

Sources: Discoveries Curve adapted from USGS/Masters, 1994. Production Curve extrapolated by author to match Discoveries volume (area under Discoveries Curve).

The global price of oil after the supply crunch should follow the simplest economic law of supply and demand: There will be a major increase in crude oil and all other fuels' prices, accompanied by global hyperinflation, rationing, etc. After the associated economic implosion, many of the world's developed societies may look like today's Russia. The United States may be competing with China for every tanker of oil, with the Persian Gulf oil exporters preferring Chinese rockets to American paper dollars for their oil.

The economic and social ramifications of the coming oil shock will require serious planning worldwide.

The global oil shortage we now can foresee will differ from the 1973 and 1979 oil-price surges, which were the result of political moves by the exporting countries. Then, global buyers began searching immediately for oil supplies during the Iran-Iraq War, which produced the world's greatest-ever oil exploration effort, from 1979 to 1985. Unfortunately, their discovery rate was much lower than earlier, and few giant fields were found. The oil field "whales" had all been fished out.

LIVING WITH LESS OIL

The first thing needed will be a U.S. tax on gasoline consumption. As Europe has done, the U.S. government should compel maximum oil conservation by imposing at least a $1 per gallon tax on gasoline. But don't expect such until a national emergency occurs. It is vehemently resisted by two groups of voters—namely, those who buy gasoline and those who sell it!

The entire world went on an "energy diet" during the 1970s by using all types of energy more efficiently (insulation, etc.), which lowered the global consumption of fuels. After 1973, the world's oil demand flattened out. Unfortunately, the global discovery rate has continued to decline precipitously, and few new non-OPEC giant fields have been found in recent years. There will be no known giant oil fields waiting to be brought on line when the next oil shortage hits about the year 2010, after which date the world's oil fields and production will steadily decline.

Figure 1 shows the type of global crude oil decline that the world can expect after the 2010 production peak. It is apparent that the use of oil products thereafter will be continually restricted. A major change in lifestyles should be expected by the lower and middle classes in all societies. Besides the government (police, armed services, etc.), only the wealthy upper classes will have the money for auto and airplane fuel.

Serious research and planning for alternative fuels will not be undertaken until governments acknowledge that a problem exists. Natural gas/methanol is an obvious existing alternative fuel that can be produced with known technologies, and almost in the huge volumes of the crude oil to be replaced (i.e., more than 1 billion gallons a day). But natural gas is already used for many other purposes, such as household and industrial heating, fertilizer, electricity, etc. So it should not be counted on to quickly replace all or most of crude oil. Building gas pipelines takes decades. The other alternative fuels (solar, wind, geothermal, wood, waste) combined produce less than 1% of U.S. electricity!

Those democratic governments in power when the global oil production peaks will all be cast out by their voters unless they have made major efforts to stave off the inevitable fuel crisis.

They have been warned!

"*World oil resources are abundant, and . . . are likely to become more so with new discoveries and changes in technology.*"

GLOBAL OIL RESERVES ARE NOT BEING EXHAUSTED

Part I: American Petroleum Institute, Part II: John L. Kennedy

In Part I of the following two-part viewpoint, the American Petroleum Institute (API) maintains that global oil reserves "are greater now than ever before." The API contends that improved exploration technology and further discoveries of oil sources will add billions of barrels of crude oil to known reserves. In Part II, John L. Kennedy argues that because of adequate reserves, expanded production capacity, and untapped oil resources, the world will not experience an oil shortage. The API is a Washington, D.C., trade association that represents America's petroleum industry. Kennedy is the editor in chief of the *Oil and Gas Journal*, a weekly petroleum industry magazine published in Houston, Texas.

As you read, consider the following questions:

1. In what depth of water can oil companies now drill, according to the API?
2. In Kennedy's opinion, how many barrels of oil could potentially be produced?
3. What is the one constant in the petroleum industry, according to Kennedy?

Part I: From the American Petroleum Institute position paper "Oil Supplies: Are We Really Running Out of Oil?" September 1996. Reprinted with permission. Part II: From John L. Kennedy, "Oil and Gas to 2000 and Beyond," speech delivered at Energy Week conference, Houston, Texas, January 1997. Reprinted by permission of the author.

I

In a sense, we are always running out of oil. Because oil is a limited resource, each barrel we produce brings us one step closer to the upper limit of oil which can be extracted.

However, we're also running into oil, discovering new reserves and developing technologies which will help us extract more from known fields.

More important, it's unlikely that our demand will ever exceed or use up our supply. As supplies grow scarce, oil prices will begin to rise, and people will turn to a more abundant, less expensive alternative. In the near term, with oil products both economical and practical, alternatives will find it hard to compete.

The shift, when it comes, won't happen overnight, because oil supplies—both conventional and unconventional—are substantial. Moreover, the change is likely to be as painless a transition as when people switched from wood to coal to heat their homes or substituted computers for typewriters to prepare letters and documents.

That's why government subsidies and mandates intended to help the nation move to approved alternatives—to "anticipate change"—are unnecessary. Government isn't needed to do what the market can and will do better and more cheaply.

World Reserves Are Substantial

World reserves are greater now than ever before. Even if we never discover another drop of oil, current reserves will be able to sustain the current rate of oil consumption for another half-century.

In 1993, the world's proved reserves were estimated to be just under a trillion barrels—about a 45-year supply of oil, based on current rates of consumption. This estimate represents a working inventory of the world's supply at a single moment in time.

Taking into account probable future oil discoveries, the U.S. Geological Survey (USGS) estimates that between 1.4 trillion and 2.1 trillion barrels of oil remain to be produced worldwide. This amount of oil would sustain the current rate of consumption between 63 to 95 years.

To be more specific, there is a 95 percent possibility that the world's remaining oil resources could last 63 more years and a 5 percent chance that the world's resources will last another 95 years at recent rates of consumption.

However, any estimate of oil reserves is somewhat uncertain. These predictions are based on current demand for petroleum products. There is no surefire way to predict future demand, although some experts predict that demand for oil will grow somewhere between 1 and 2 percent annually.

TECHNOLOGICAL PROGRESS FORESTALLS EXHAUSTION

Our oil supply also depends critically on technology. The amount of resources remaining is fixed, but only in the way that a rubber band is fixed. The world's production capacity can be expanded with better technology.

New exploration techniques are already improving the scope and success of offshore drilling operations, adding to the world's known resources.

For example, in 1965, the petroleum industry's drilling capabilities limited offshore wells to waters less than 300 feet deep. Today, the industry drills for oil in waters as deep as 3,000 feet.

One new technology is three-dimensional seismic analysis. Using traditional seismic analysis, the industry successfully completed just over 40 percent of new wells. With 3-D seismic analysis, that success rate has risen to over 70 percent.

Such advances are crucial to the lifespan of the world's oil supply, because every 1 percent increase in the industry's average recovery rate can add between 60 billion and 80 billion barrels to resource estimates. That's enough to last three to four years, based on current rates of consumption.

And, if economically feasible ways to extract and refine unconventional sources of oil are found, our oil supply could be extended for hundreds of years. A large part of the world's remaining resources is found in the form of oil shales, heavy and extra heavy oils and bitumins. These unconventional resources are equal in volume to ten times the amount of recoverable conventional oil resources that remain.

POTENTIAL FOR MORE DISCOVERIES

The good news is that world oil resources are abundant, and, if anything, are likely to become more so with new discoveries and changes in technology. However, major new investment will be needed to translate this potential into production—and, in most of the world's largest producing countries, there has been stagnation or deterioration in the investment climate. That's because, at home as well as abroad, barriers stand in the way of full resource extraction.

At home, the area that has been called "the best single opportunity to increase significantly domestic oil production" by the U.S. Department of the Interior—the coastal plain of the Arctic National Wildlife Refuge—is closed to drilling, despite the fact that the department found that there is a 46 percent chance of discovering economically recoverable oil, possibly totaling several billion barrels.

NOT MEANINGFULLY FINITE

The oil potential of a particular well may be measured, and hence it is limited (though it is interesting and relevant that as we develop new ways of extracting hard-to-get oil, the economic capacity of a well increases). But the number of wells that will eventually produce oil, and in what quantities, is not known or measurable at present and probably never will be, and hence is not meaningfully finite.

Julian L. Simon, *The Ultimate Resource 2*, 1996.

And internationally, institutional and other barriers threaten the realization of full production potential. For example, in Russia, ambiguous property rights and political turmoil add risks. Oil developed in the newly independent states of the former Soviet Union must be transported through volatile or politically hostile territory in order to reach its destination.

Political volatility also remains an obstacle to new investment in the Middle East. Territorial disputes, shifting alliances and issues of succession cloud the future of investments in this crucial region.

II

For the rest of the twentieth century and into the next, world demand for natural gas and petroleum products will grow at a healthy pace. Reserves are adequate, producing capacity can be expanded, and markets for oil and oil products are sophisticated and efficient.

Crude oil is a world commodity and natural gas is becoming a commodity in the large North American and European markets. Like other commodity markets, the markets for oil and natural gas are marked by short term volatility.

Despite this volatility, plentiful reserves and the ability of technology to lower exploitation costs will keep a lid on long term oil and gas prices.

Energy users, as well as oil and gas producers, refiners, and sellers need a solid understanding of these fundamentals of energy supply and demand. Energy consumers and producers also need an understanding of how today's oil and natural gas markets work.

Crude oil markets are global. Prices are much the same anywhere in the world after adjusting for quality differences and transportation costs. However, the price of petroleum products—gasoline, diesel, residual fuel—varies widely among countries, depending primarily on the tax rate. As governments wrestle with social, economic, and environmental challenges, taxes are likely to account for an even bigger share of the retail cost of petroleum products.

Natural gas markets are more regional because it is not so easily and cheaply transported. Still, in large unregulated markets like the U.S., natural gas prices can also fluctuate over a wide range. Though the North American market is a leader in deregulating gas supply and transportation services, other regions will gradually make natural gas and other energy markets more competitive.

HEALTHY DEMAND

Long term petroleum market fundamentals are clear: supplies are adequate and world demand will continue to grow steadily. Adequate supplies ensure that prices will not increase significantly, on average, till the end of the 1990s, probably beyond.

Most forecasters expect worldwide petroleum demand to grow at about 1.5% until 2010. World Bank predicts oil demand growth will average 1.6% per year between 1994 and 2010.

Economic growth will be the key to energy demand and economic growth will be much faster in the developing countries than in the mature economies. The International Energy Agency [IEA] estimates world economic growth between 1992 and 2010 will average 3.1% per year. OECD [Organization for Economic Cooperation and Development] will grow at 2.5%, FSU [former Soviet Union] and central European economies at 2.1%.

The rest of the world—Latin America, Africa, Middle East, East Asia, South Asia, and China—will grow at an average rate of 5.3%. China's economy will grow at almost 8% per year. Throughout developing countries in Asia, Latin America, and elsewhere, demand for transportation fuels will boom as the car population balloons. As per capita income rises, so will demand for petrochemical products.

World natural gas demand will grow faster than oil demand. Under its "capacity constraints" case, IEA estimates world natural gas demand will increase 2.5% per year from 1992 to 2010.

It will not all be clear sailing. Downward pressure on oil and gas demand could result from efforts to reduce fossil fuels consumption for environmental reasons. So far, this pressure has been in the form of additional taxes aimed at reducing CO_2 [carbon dioxide] emissions. When this pressure takes the form of carbon taxes, natural gas has an advantage over oil products.

SHORT TERM VOLATILITY

Long term averages are one thing, but business planners must deal with another market reality. Oil prices will continue to be volatile because productive capacity will not always move in step with demand. The good news for energy users and producers is that there are new ways to manage risk in oil and gas markets. Petroleum futures and options trading in the U.S., Europe, and Asia provide liquidity and flexibility for buyers and sellers.

The combination of demand and productive capacity—the ability to get oil and gas from the reservoir to the consumer—sets short term prices. When demand grows, producers who have adequate reserves will expand capacity. When excess capacity is fully utilized, prices will rise until capacity is again expanded.

Tens of billions of dollars will be needed through the year 2005 to expand producing capacity. Most of these expansions will be in the oil producing countries in the Middle East.

PLENTIFUL SUPPLY

The world's proven conventional crude oil reserves are about 1 trillion barrels, enough to last 46 years at today's consumption levels. State oil companies own almost three-fourths of these reserves; two-thirds are in the Middle East.

Another 8–9 trillion barrels of oil could come from oil sands, tar sands, enhanced oil recovery efforts, and new discoveries. Most of this additional oil is not competitive with conventional oil at today's prices, but there are exceptions.

The cost of producing Alberta's [a Canadian province] tar sands, for example, is nearing a level that makes it competitive with conventional crude oil in today's market.

Worldwide reserves of natural gas are plentiful, too, totaling about 4,900 trillion cubic feet. At today's consumption rates, that is more than a 60-year supply.

DEALING WITH CHANGE

Every aspect of the worldwide petroleum industry has changed since the mid-1980s. To survive the market upheavals since then, oil and gas companies around the world have changed the way they operate and the work they do. Restructuring, outsourcing, and partnering will continue as increasing costs and flat prices squeeze profits.

Energy use patterns will change. Fuel and other product specifications will change. Market shares of oil and gas will shift.

One constant throughout these changes—in all regions and in all industry segments—will be fierce competition. There will be competition for markets and for capital, for jobs, for ideas, for profit. There will be competition among energy sources, among producing countries, among exploration companies, among refiners.

Globalization of the industry will continue to intensify this competition. All over the world, companies are going beyond their national borders, sticking their noses into markets that others thought they had to themselves.

In the years ahead, there will be new players in every region around the world in every business. Opportunities abound in this new market environment. Growing markets always provide opportunities. Technology has helped operators dramatically lower finding, developing, and producing costs. Technology has helped companies do more work with fewer people. It has helped producers and users of oil and gas manage price risk in volatile markets.

Just as important as technology are creative approaches to relationships with customers, suppliers, and competitors. Creativity in organization is just as important as innovative technology.

No one in the worldwide petroleum industry should be waiting for the industry to get back to "normal." This is normal. This is reality. This is the business and market environment we will operate in for the next 20 years.

The petroleum industry does not need a scarcity or supply interruption to prosper. It should not expect one; it should not even want one. The petroleum age is far from being over. Supplies are plentiful and vast resources remain untapped. Oil and gas will continue to provide more than half the world's energy for a long time to come.

Growing markets, adequate supply, affordable products, and a 60% market share are the signs of an industry with a bright future. That solid foundation and the international petroleum industry's demonstrated ability to adapt to market conditions make it able to supply tomorrow's growing markets with affordable energy.

| "Food scarcity is likely to emerge as the defining issue of the era now beginning."

FOOD SUPPLIES ARE BECOMING SCARCER

Lester R. Brown

Lester R. Brown is the president of the Worldwatch Institute, an environmental research organization in Washington, D.C. In the following viewpoint, Brown argues that food supplies are shrinking worldwide. According to Brown, this decrease in food supplies has been caused chiefly by the fact that grain production has increased only 3 percent since 1990, while world grain stocks have dropped to their lowest level ever. Also contributing to scarcer food supplies are population growth, extreme weather conditions, land and water scarcity, soil erosion, and industrialization, Brown maintains.

As you read, consider the following questions:

1. By how much does human population increase annually, according to Brown?
2. According to the author, what types of food are grown on irrigated land?
3. According to Brown, what are the three reserves that the world can draw upon in the event of poor grain harvests?

From *Tough Choices: Facing the Challenge of Food Scarcity* by Lester R. Brown. Copyright ©1996 by Worldwatch Institute. Reprinted by permission of W. W. Norton & Company, Inc.

During the late spring and early summer of 1996, world wheat and corn prices set record highs. Wheat traded at over $7 a bushel, more than double the price in early 1995. In mid-July, corn traded at an all-time price of $5.54 a bushel, also more than twice the level of a year earlier.

These startlingly high prices were the result of production falling behind demand. During the nineties, the growth in world grain production has slowed dramatically, while demand has continued to climb, driven by the addition of nearly 90 million people a year and an unprecedented rise in affluence in Asia, led by China. Part of this widening gap has been filled in recent years by drawing down carryover stocks—the amount left in the world's grain bins at the start of each new harvest. By 1996, these had fallen to 50 days of consumption, the lowest level on record.

Several trends are converging to create scarcity and raise prices. With all oceanic fisheries being fished at or beyond capacity, growth in the oceanic fish catch came to a halt in 1989. For the first time in history, farmers can no longer count on getting any help from fishers in expanding the food supply. Yet there is little new cropland to bring under the plow, and a growing scarcity of fresh water for irrigation. In many countries, efforts to raise land productivity are handicapped by the physiological inability of existing varieties of grain to use more fertilizer than is already being applied.

In addition, farmers who have always had to cope with the vagaries of weather may now be dealing with climate change. The 11 warmest years since recordkeeping began in 1866 have all occurred since 1979. In fact, the three warmest years took place during the nineties, with 1995 topping the list. Unfortunately for farmers and consumers, crop-withering heat waves like those that shrank harvests in 1995 across the United States, Canada, several European countries, the Ukraine, and Russia could become even more frequent and intense if atmospheric carbon dioxide (CO_2) levels continue to build.

At the same time that the growth in grain production is slowing, the growth in demand is accelerating. In addition to trying to feed nearly 90 million more people each year, farmers now face a record rise in affluence in Asia—home to more than half the world's people. A large share of Asia's 3.1 billion people are moving up the food chain, eating more pork, poultry, beef, and eggs and drinking more beer, all of which are grain-intensive products. . . .

Growth in the harvest from the land has continued during the nineties, but at a much slower rate than during the preceding decades. From 1950 to 1990, the world grain harvest increased from 631 million tons to 1,780 million tons, nearly tripling. This was a remarkable period in history, one in which rapidly growing demand driven by record growth in both population and incomes stimulated production increases as farmers drew on a huge backlog of technology developed during the preceding century. Since 1990, however, the growth in the grain harvest has slowed dramatically. After expanding 182 percent from 1950 to 1990, the harvest has increased only 3 percent between 1990 and 1996. Signs of a slowdown in growth in grain production were already evident in the late eighties as the grain harvest per person fell from the all-time high of 346 kilograms in 1984 to 336 kilograms in 1990, a drop of 3 percent. By 1996, the harvest per person had fallen to 313 kilograms, declining an additional 7 percent.

With this loss of momentum in the growth in the world grain harvest since 1990, it comes as no surprise that world grain stocks during the nineties have dropped to their lowest level ever.

WORLD GRAIN CARRYOVER STOCKS AS DAYS OF CONSUMPTION, 1961–96

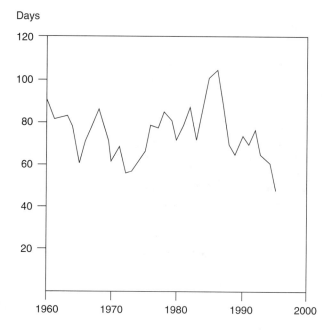

Source: United States Department of Agriculture.

The bumper harvest of 1990 boosted carryover stocks for 1991 to 342 million tons. But during the years since then they have dropped to 240 million tons—a mere 50 days of consumption.

In response to the tightening grain situation, in 1996 the United States released for production the remaining land held out under commodity set-aside programs. Yet even with this additional land, there will be little rebuilding of stocks from the 1996 harvest.

In some ways, carryover stocks of grain are the most sensitive indicator of food security. Stocks that will provide at least 70 days of world consumption are needed for even a minimal level of food security. Whenever they fall below 60 days, prices become highly volatile. With the margin of security so thin, grain prices fluctuate with each weather report. When carryover stocks of grain dropped to 55 days of consumption in 1973, for example, world grain prices doubled. When they reached the new low of 50 days of consumption in 1996, the world price of wheat and corn—the two leading grains in terms of quantity produced—again more than doubled.

Another factor affecting future world food security is the share of current food production that is based on the unsustainable use of land and water. For example, a small fraction of the world's cropland is so highly erodible that it cannot sustain cultivation over the long term. A few countries have attempted to calculate the share of their harvest in this category. In Kazakstan, a wheat-exporting country, for instance, the Institute of Soil Management estimates that its grainland area will be reduced by one fourth or more when the rapidly eroding land now under cultivation is eventually abandoned as its productivity falls.

A similar situation exists with irrigation water use. For example, the U.S. Department of Agriculture reports that 21 percent of U.S. irrigated cropland is being watered by drawing down underground aquifers. In northern China, the limited information that is available suggests that farmers may depend even more on overpumping. No one knows precisely what share of the world grain harvest is based on the unsustainable use of land and water, but the inevitable abandonment of eroding cropland and the depletion of aquifers both threaten future food security.

So do rising atmospheric levels of greenhouse gases, which are linked to higher temperatures and more extreme weather events, including droughts, floods, crop-withering heat waves, and more powerful, more destructive storms. If the earth's average temperature continues to rise over the next 15 years at the same rate it has during the last 15, more intense crop-withering heat waves—like those that lowered world harvests in 1988 and 1995—could take an even heavier toll on future grain harvests. The experience in 1988 shows that intense heat and drought can totally eliminate the exportable surplus of grain in the United States, the world's breadbasket. If that were to happen at a time when grain stocks were already depleted, as they are now, it would drive the price of grain off the charts, creating chaos in world markets.

Given the slowdown in the growth of the oceanic fish catch and the world grain harvest, meeting the food needs of the nearly 90 million people being added each year is now achieved in part by reducing consumption among those already here. If the sustainable-yield limits of the oceans have been reached, the only way to arrest the decline in the per capita fish catch and the accompanying rise in seafood prices is to stabilize world population size. And while there are still innumerable opportunities for expanding the world grain harvest, it is becoming difficult to sustain rapid growth. Unfortunately, the situation is likely to get worse before it gets better.

LAND AND WATER SCARCITY

As the world's population, now approaching 5.8 billion, continues to expand, both the area of cropland and the amount of fresh water per person are shrinking, threatening to drop below the level needed to provide minimal levels of food security. Over time, farmers have used ingenious methods to expand the area used to produce crops. These included irrigation, terracing, drainage, fallowing, and even, for the Dutch, reclaiming land from the sea. Terracing let farmers cultivate steeply sloping land on a sustainable basis, quite literally enabling them to farm the mountains as well as the plains. Drainage of wetlands opened fertile bottomlands for cultivation. Alternate-year fallowing to accumulate moisture helped farmers extend cropping into semi-arid regions.

By mid-century, the frontiers of agricultural settlement had largely disappeared, contributing to a dramatic slowdown in the growth in area planted to grain, the source of half of human caloric intake consumed directly and a substantial share of the remainder consumed indirectly in the form of meat, milk, and eggs. Between 1950 and 1981, the grain area increased from 587 million hectares to 732 million hectares, a gain of nearly 25 percent. But part of the expansion was on land that was subject to severe soil erosion by wind or water, much of it in the former Soviet Union. The peak Soviet grain area of 123 million hectares in 1979 shrank to 91 million hectares in 1995, declining almost every year during this 18-year stretch, as falling productivity forced the abandonment of marginal, often heavily eroded, land.

In the United States, a more formal effort was made to rescue the highly erodible land that was plowed in response to the high grain prices of the mid-seventies. In 1985, Congress, with the strong support of environmental groups, passed the Conservation Reserve Program, an initiative designed to retire much of this land by paying farmers to return it to grass before it became wasteland. By 1990, some 14 million hectares had been set aside under long-term contracts.

In addition to soil erosion, another leading source of cropland loss is industrialization, a trend that is strongest in countries already densely populated when rapid industrialization gets under way. The subsequent changes claim large amounts of land for the construction of factories and warehouses, as does the evolution of an automobile-centered transportation system. . . .

IRRIGATION

In addition to land scarcity, farmers are now facing water scarcity. The expanding demand for water is pushing beyond the sustainable yield of aquifers in many countries and is draining some of the world's major rivers dry before they reach the sea. As the demand for water for irrigation and for industrial and residential uses continues to expand, the competition between countryside and city for available water supplies intensifies. In some parts of the world, meeting growing urban needs is possible only by diverting water from irrigation.

One of the keys to the near tripling of the world grain harvest from 1950 to 1990 was a 2.5-fold expansion of irrigation, a development that extended agriculture into arid regions with little rainfall, intensified production in low-rainfall areas, and increased dry-season cropping in countries with monsoonal climates. It also accounts for part of the phenomenal growth in world fertilizer use since mid-century. Most of the world's rice and much of its wheat is produced on irrigated land.

From the beginning of irrigation several thousand years ago until 1900, irrigated area expanded slowly, eventually covering some 40 million hectares. From 1900 to 1950, the pace picked up, and the total area more than doubled to 94 million hectares. But the big growth occurred from 1950 to 1993, when 154 million hectares were added, bringing the total to 248 million hectares.

During this period, a key threshold was crossed in 1979. From 1950 until then, irrigation expanded faster than population, increasing the irrigated area per person by nearly one third. This was closely associated with a worldwide rise in grain production per person of one third. But since 1979, the growth in irrigation has fallen behind that of population, shrinking the irrigated area per person by some 7 percent. This trend, now well established, will undoubtedly continue as the demand for water presses ever more tightly against available supplies. . . .

DEALING WITH FOOD SCARCITY

Until recently, the world had three reserves it could call on in the event of a poor harvest: cropland idled under farm programs; surplus stocks of grain in storage; and the one third of the world grain harvest that is fed to livestock, poultry, and fish. As of early 1997, two of these reserves—the idled cropland and the surplus stocks—have largely disappeared. The only remaining reserve that can be tapped in a world food emergency is the grain used as feed. This is much more difficult to draw on. Higher prices, of course, will move the world's affluent down the food chain. But they also threaten the survival of the world's low-income consumers. . . .

If this analysis is at all close to the mark, then food scarcity is likely to emerge as the defining issue of the era now beginning, much as ideological conflict was the defining issue of the historical era that recently ended. National political leaders everywhere will be thoroughly challenged by the new demands placed on them by the prospect of growing food scarcity. Ensuring the food security of the next generation requires fundamental changes in population policy, energy policy, land use policy, water use policy, and, indeed, in the very definition of national security itself. Whether or not political leaders can respond quickly enough to avoid widespread political instability remains to be seen.

| "Grain yields have continued a steady and nearly constant increase over the last several decades in both the First and Third Worlds."

FOOD SUPPLIES ARE NOT BECOMING SCARCER

Dennis T. Avery

Dennis T. Avery, a former U.S. Department of Agriculture policy analyst, is the director of global food issues at the conservative Hudson Institute research organization in Indianapolis. In the following viewpoint, Avery disputes environmentalists' claims that the world is threatened by the prospect of food shortages and famines. According to Avery, global grain production has been increasing for more than a century, and "the current world food situation is the best ever." He maintains that biotechnology, improved agricultural techniques, and millions of acres of underutilized or wasted farmland can be further exploited to increase crop yields.

As you read, consider the following questions:

1. What will be the world's peak population in the twenty-first century, according to the Winrock Foundation, cited by Avery?
2. According to Avery, what two factors could substantially increase the world's demand for food?
3. In the author's opinion, what has enabled the world to avoid transforming wildlands into farmland?

From Dennis T. Avery, "The Myth of Global Hunger." This article appeared in the January 1997 issue and is reprinted with permission from the World & I, a publication of The Washington Times Corporation; copyright ©1997.

Twenty-five years ago, an alarm was sounded: We faced a global food crisis. Many predicted that the world was entering an age of food shortages, high prices, and large-scale famines.

These dire forecasts were followed by a call for radical population-control programs, under the assumption that it would be difficult if not impossible to increase farming yields enough to feed the burgeoning population.

Lester Brown, for example, in his 1974 book *By Bread Alone*, warned ominously, "The choice is between famine and family planning."

But while the food-shortage and famine prophesies have yet to come true, recent years have seen a renewal of these predictions, spurred by two current trends:

• Global grain stocks, used as reserves in years of short harvest or high demand, fell to a near-record low in 1995–96 of only 45 days of consumption.

• The economic success of many Third World countries, especially in Asia, is giving large populations the individual incomes they need to upgrade their diets. As more people eat more meat, the world's demand for feed grains increases.

Are the famine forecasters correct this time? Or are they continuing to misread the world's rising ability to feed itself?

LOW WORLD GRAIN STOCKS

The fact that world grain stocks have reached a modern low point has little to do with population growth and has virtually no implications at all for famine.

In 1995, several factors led to the low-stocks situation. That year saw (1) poor harvests in America's grain belt, (2) an increase in feed grain use in China and other economically emerging countries, and, most important, (3) a change in U.S. farm policy.

For 60 years, American farm policy tried to keep world grain prices higher than the market would support. In most years, that stuck America with up to 400 million tons of "surplus" grain. The rest of the world benefited from U.S. carryover stocks but was all too willing to let America pay the costs. The only other significant grain stocks have been held by the European Union [EU], which was also trying to keep its farmers' grain prices high.

Over the past several years, however, budget deficits have forced both the United States and the EU to cut back the amount of grain held in carryover stocks. In 1996, America finally took the radical step of scrapping its price-support system altogether. This would have triggered momentous change in world grain markets under any circumstances, but it happened right after

America's 1995 grain crops were sharply reduced by both bad weather and millions of acres of ill-advised cropland diversion spurred by the government.

Nineteen ninety-six also happened to be the year that China's rising affluence (and thus rising meat demand) forced it to forgo its usual 10 million tons of corn exports and import 5 million tons of corn instead.

Added together, these factors led to the low grain stocks situation in 1995–96. The paucity is only temporary, however, because high prices have whetted the enthusiasm of farmers all over the world. . . .

In the 1960s, when world population was rising by nearly 2.1 percent per year and crop production in the developing countries was barely gaining 1 percent annually, global food shortages were, perhaps, a plausible forecast.

These trends, however, have radically changed.

World Never So Well Fed

Even before the alarms were sounded, efforts were under way to improve the agricultural situation in the Third World. During the 1960s, an international network of agricultural researchers and research centers began extending across the globe the benefits of the green revolution: the scientific strides that have sent crop yields through the silo roof.

By the early 1970s, farm output in the Third World was rising at well over 2 percent annually, and the population growth rate was beginning to moderate.

The current world food situation is the best ever. Total calories per capita have risen by about one-third since 1960, and virtually everyone outside of Africa now has at least a minimally adequate calorie intake. (Africa's problem is bad government, not a lack of farming resources or even agricultural technology. Its current corn yields average less than 0.32 tons per acre but should be four times that high.)

This is not to argue that the food situation has been resolved for every person on earth. The world still has roughly 800 million chronically "food insecure" individuals, according to the International Food Policy Research Institute. However, this classification encompasses many degrees of food-access difficulty, and being moderately "food insecure" is much better than being an actual famine victim.

The famines of the last two decades have either resulted from civil war or been confined to the harshest, most uncertain, and thinly populated regions of Africa, or both.

The hunger remaining in the world is not due to distribution problems. Simple poverty is to blame. The bitter irony is that most countries have adequate agricultural resources to produce their own basic food supplies, if they use high-yield seeds and fertilizers (Africa mostly doesn't) and if they adopt effective government institutions that don't rob the people and discourage farmers and industries.

While acknowledging the success in overall world food production over the last 30 years, where is the world heading? Have the neo-Malthusians [named after British economist Thomas Malthus, who theorized that population would grow faster than food supplies and lead to famine and war] been right all along, only premature in their predictions? To answer this question, we need to evaluate trends in the components that contribute to food production and demand: crop yields, farmland availability, population growth, input constraints (for example, irrigation water), and food consumption patterns.

POPULATION IS STABILIZING RAPIDLY

The pessimists' biggest fear has been planetary overpopulation. The idea of growing beyond the carrying capacity of the planet originated with the concept of a limited food supply. Consequently, population control has been virtually their only policy solution.

The problem with population management is that it is nearly powerless to stop population growth suddenly. A growing population is like a long train with a lot of momentum. Contraceptives make only about a 10 percent difference in the effectiveness of families' birth-control decisions.

The good news is that, although the world has largely ignored the recommendations for drastic population-control programs, the World Bank notes that the world's population growth rate fell from 2.2 percent per year in the 1960s to 1.8 percent in the 1970s. The current growth rate is 1.6 percent per year.

Instead of world population spiraling ever upward, out of control, we are seeing a onetime surge—due to modern medicine and lower death rates—that is rapidly tapering off.

The main reason the world's population growth rate is declining so fast is that the average number of births per woman (bpw) in the Third World is down from 6.1 in 1965 to 3.1 today, according to the World Bank.

A population remains stable at an average of 2.1 bpw, which means the Third World has come three-fourths of the way to stability in one generation. Most affluent countries level off at 1.7

or 1.8 bpw, which means the world's population will eventually peak and then slowly decline.

The world's current population is estimated at nearly 6 billion. According to a study conducted by the Winrock Foundation, the peak world population will be less than 9 billion people, reached around 2040. We won't get more than that, because the brakes have already been applied on the population train. It just takes a while to fully stop it.

Brighter Food Prospects

Food productivity per worker and per acre have improved thanks to power machinery and biological innovations induced by increased demand, the improved ability of farmers to get their produce to market on better transportation systems, and, most importantly, expanding economic freedom. . . .

Food prospects grow brighter still due to genetic manipulation of plants and better methods of irrigating, cultivating and fertilizing. But even without the further progress that is sure to come, the future is assured for farmland and food.

Julian L. Simon, *Wall Street Journal*, November 18, 1996.

Besides population growth, one other major trend will add to the world's food demand: affluence. As free trade and economic growth spread around the globe, the world's poor are getting more affluent. Along with income growth comes the desire and purchasing power for more affluent diets: more meat, milk, eggs, and dairy products.

These foods take two to five times as many farming resources per calorie to produce as grains do. So when populations start eating more meat and milk, they are effectively consuming significantly higher quantities of grain and agricultural resources.

Combined, population growth and affluence will probably double the world's food demand and possibly triple it. Can countries meet this challenge?

THE DOOMSAYERS ARE WRONG

The world's grain production has been increasing for over a century. According to U.S. Department of Agriculture statistics, world grain production has increased linearly since 1950.

Brown and other pessimists point to the years [1992–1996] as evidence that production is reaching its upper limits. But they have made similar claims following periodic production drops in the past. Actually, this last production plateau is almost entirely due to the collapse of economic and farming systems in the former Soviet Union. The true trend has yet to be interrupted.

Pessimists such as Brown worry that humankind is losing farmland to roads, homes, and shopping malls. But the world will not suffer a food crisis because of urban development.

Cities currently occupy roughly 1.5 percent of the earth's surface. According to a World Bank study, even at the peak world population, cities will occupy less than 4 percent of the total land area. Considering the expected food needs, specialists would have to fail miserably in their efforts to increase crop yields and in the other agricultural policy areas for this small loss to push humankind over the brink into food crisis.

Moreover, the world has millions of acres of good farmland in the United States, Argentina, and western Europe that are underutilized or even wasted.

The doomsayers believe that the world won't be able to increase crop yields substantially. Nations are now experiencing the biological and practical limits to their ability to increase crop yields, the pessimists claim.

"Unfortunately, the inability of agricultural scientists to come up with a new formula to boost output means that production has stalled," says Brown in *State of the World: 1996*.

Actually, Brown made similar claims in 1989 and, remarkably, even way back in 1974. Yet grain yields have continued a steady and nearly constant increase over the last several decades in both the First and Third Worlds.

And the future looks bright for increasing crop yields. Traditional breeding techniques have been given new life by the science and tools of molecular biology. Using gene identification and marking techniques, tissue culture, and a host of other technologies, plant breeders can achieve years of traditional breeding advances in only a season or two.

Biotechnology holds even greater promise. Disease-resistant and drought-tolerant varieties are just the beginning. Researchers are redesigning virtually the whole layout of some plants, increasing the size of grain heads while shortening and strengthening the stalks to support them.

There is much reason for optimism.

SAVING NATURE WITH HIGH-YIELD FARMING

The real issue is not whether the world will experience massive food shortages in the future. According to the evidence, it almost certainly will not. The real question is whether humankind will spare room for nature as we feed ourselves.

This is actually one of the pessimists' major concerns. Paul Ehrlich, noted author of *The Population Bomb*, believes humankind has already surpassed the earth's carrying capacity. Yet his real concern is preserving habitat for wildlife.

SAVING WILDLIFE

The environmental movement is strident in its belief that population control is needed to save wildlife habitat from human encroachment. But if environmentalists are truly worried about wildlife and realize the realistic limitations on population-control measures, then maximizing land-use efficiency is essential. Nowhere is that more important than in agriculture.

According to the UN Food and Agriculture Organization, farming already occupies over a third of the earth's land area. In reality, modern, high-yield farming—which environmental activists ironically despise—has saved an enormous amount of the world's wildlife.

In recent decades, the world has lost hardly any of its wildlands to population growth, because nations have been increasing crop yields rather than plowing down wild forests. The world has been cropping nearly the same 5.8 million square miles of land since the end of World War II.

NO LAND LOSS

The world today still has about one-third of its land area in forests, just as it had 35 years ago, because nations haven't had to take more land for food. Without the higher yields produced with hybrid seeds, irrigation, fertilizers, and pesticides, the world would have already lost another 10–12 million square miles of wildlands. That's equal to the total land area of the United States, Europe, and Brazil combined!

Fortunately, the vast majority of the world's biodiversity is still out there to be saved—in the tropical forests and the mountain microclimates. The earth hasn't really begun to lose big tracts of wildlands yet.

Ultimately, the dilemma is that nations will have to either triple the yields on existing croplands or take huge tracts of land from nature.

If the world goes the route of increasing yields based on high-powered seeds, trees, and irrigation technologies, experts say 90-plus percent of the wildlands can be saved—and an even higher percentage of the wildlife species.

The food-supply pessimists have never wavered from their

claims that humanity would soon hit the limits to the earth's bounty. Despite repeatedly failed predictions of disaster and continuing demonstrations of human ingenuity and adaptability, they believe the good times have passed.

Yet, looking at the trends in population growth, crop yields, land use, and food demand, the doomsday scenarios seem less likely with every passing year.

| "There are many . . . countries in which rain forests and the areas around them are under siege."

RAIN FOREST DESTRUCTION HAS REACHED CRISIS PROPORTIONS

Arthur Golden and Matt Miller

Late in 1993, *San Diego Union-Tribune* journalists traveled to Central America and Southeast Asia to investigate the clear-cutting of tropical rain forests. In the following viewpoint, published February 2, 1994, *Union-Tribune* staff writers Arthur Golden and Matt Miller argue that unabated rain forest cutting—much of it by loggers and migrant farmers who harvest valuable mahogany—is damaging precious rain forest areas. Such deforestation, the authors assert, is responsible for devastating floods and mudslides that have killed thousands of people. According to Golden and Miller, officials fear that rain forest cutting will cause irreversible environmental damage.

As you read, consider the following questions:

1. According to Golden and Miller, how much of the world's rain forests are destroyed annually?
2. Why are some rain forests less endangered by deforestation than others, in the authors' opinion?
3. According to Rafael Leonardo Callejas, cited by the authors, what is the only way to preserve rain forests?

Reprinted from Arthur Golden and Matt Miller, "The Vanishing Rain Forest," *San Diego Union-Tribune*, February 2, 1994, by permission of the *San Diego Union-Tribune*.

Near a mountaintop in a remote Honduran rain forest, the first act of a global tragedy is under way.

Just below the summit, two men struggle to cut a felled mahogany tree into chunks small enough to be hauled away on mule-back. Alejandro Hernández and his brother, Francisco, heave their 5-foot-long manual saw through the tree. The brothers work barefoot in a rainstorm that sends rivers of mud cascading down the mountain. The rain crackles like volleys of rifle fire as it lashes a bending canopy of leaves overhead.

In six days of grueling, dangerous labor on the mountain, the brothers will earn about $60 apiece. By the time the timber has been crafted into mahogany furniture, that same wood will fetch thousands of dollars at retail stores in the United States, Europe and Japan.

For the brothers and their families, the tree they have destroyed represents economic survival. But for other people, even those appalled at the terrible poverty that shrouds life in places like Honduras, the destruction of a single mahogany tree profanes the emerald majesty of the rain forest and jeopardizes the very future of mankind.

Nineteen months have elapsed since world leaders convened a headline-grabbing Earth Summit in Brazil that was designed to help save the rain forests. There is no doubt that the conference succeeded in raising international awareness about the importance of rain forests. As a practical matter, however, deforestation continues to drive rain forest plants, birds, mammals and insects into extinction at a pace even faster than that of the disappearance of dinosaurs hundreds of millions of years ago, said environmental biologist David Woodruff of the University of California, San Diego.

Woodruff and other scientists and environmentalists paint an apocalyptic picture of the world without rain forests. Elimination of the forests could unleash titanic changes in global climatic conditions, kill off plants that promise cures for countless diseases and increase the possibility of outright warfare between nations whose natural resources have been devastated.

The brothers sawing the tree on the Honduran mountain are symbols of an epic battle in tropical areas around the world over the fate of rain forests. The battle pits federal governments against their most impoverished citizens, as well as against wealthy and influential loggers and ranchers. All want to squeeze profit from the land—often despite laws that prohibit or severely limit its exploitation.

A Fact-Finding Trek

Late last year, *Union-Tribune* journalists trekked through rain forests in Honduras and Guatemala in Central America, and Malaysia and the Philippines in Southeast Asia. Those journeys were supported by weeks of additional research and interviews with a wide range of rain-forest-related experts around the world. The focus of the investigation was mahogany, the tropical timber that is central to the struggle over the rain forest and that is prized by consumers from San Diego to Tokyo.

The findings were hardly encouraging. While attention is most often centered on the huge, troubled Amazon River rain forest of Brazil, there are many other countries in which rain forests and the areas around them are under siege. Often, those forests escape international scrutiny almost entirely. Yet they, too, are now swarming with small-scale farmers and their families—destitute migrants, often forgotten by their governments, whose only goal is survival. Most critically, the migrants generally use primitive farming methods that exhaust the rain forests' natural resources.

The number of people worldwide who have encroached on rain forests is believed to have soared from 200 million in 1970 to at least 500 million today, said Norman Myers, an ecologist-demographer at Oxford University in England. The forest-land migrant phenomenon "thus represents the biggest mass movement of people in such a short time in the history of mankind," he said.

Rain forest destruction, estimated at some 35 million acres worldwide each year, has hardly slowed since then-President Bush and other statesmen declared at the June 1992 Earth Summit in Rio de Janeiro that rain forest preservation was an urgent international priority.

Proposals abound for striking a balance between utilizing rain forest resources and saving them. But execution of those programs takes time and money, commodities that are lacking in most rain forest nations.

There are a few rays of hope. Generally, however, the outlook is bleak.

"We have now lost about half the world's tropical rain forests," said Myers. While rain forests in the western Amazon region of Brazil, the Zaire basin in central Africa and the South Pacific island of New Guinea appear safe for the time being because they are too far from population centers and markets and too wet for most agriculture. Myers said he "can't see all that much hope" for rain forests in most other locations.

STAGGERING LOSSES

One of the most critical areas for tropical deforestation is the La-candón rain forest in southern Mexico, mostly in the state of Chiapas, where Mayan farmers launched a spectacular armed rebellion last month that was generated in part by a desperate search for farmland. Myers estimated that 10 percent—a staggering 3,000 square miles—of the already decimated Lacandón forest is being destroyed each year.

At that rate, the 30,000 square miles of rain forest remaining in the Lacandón would be denuded in 10 years.

The outlook in Central America is just as gloomy. Dr. Carlos A. Medina, a physician who took office in July as Honduras' first minister of the environment, said 50 acres of his Tennessee-size nation's rain forests are being destroyed every hour.

CAUSES OF RAIN FOREST CUTTING

Worldwide, the tropical forest shrank by about 142,000 square kilometers per year in the early nineties. Of that amount, about 80,000 square kilometers fell to slash-and-burn agriculture. Another 10,000 square kilometers were deforested by the search for fuelwood. Forest clearing for cattle ranching, mostly in Brazil and Central America, took another 15,000 square kilometers per year. Unduly destructive logging methods, primarily in Southeast Asia took another 25,000 square kilometers annually. Large dams, mining, and road building projects removed another 10,000 square kilometers, while forest clearing for tea, rubber, and oil palm plantations took about 5,000.

Malcolm Gillis, *Vital Speeches of the Day*, April 1, 1996.

"If nothing positive is done in defense of our rain forests, we calculate that between the years 2010 and 2020, Honduras will become a desert," Medina said. "That would mean that Honduras' current level of poverty will sink into misery and that our nation will descend into a catastrophic economic situation, possibly like that of Ethiopia or Somalia."

In a worst-case scenario, said President Ramiro de León Carpio of neighboring Guatemala, the death of rain forests would generate irreversible worldwide environmental damage.

"Rain forests are the natural lungs of mankind," de Leon said. "If we fail to preserve the rain forests, more people will die than have perished in world wars. It would be the worst blot that humanity could have. Without rain forests, people are going to fight over a patch of shade, a little bit of water, the kind of environment that permits them to live—and that is going to be fatal."

But for all their good intentions, tropical nations lack a basic ingredient in environmental protection—money. Striking a theme that was repeated in countless interviews with officials and environmental workers, de León said Guatemala has very little money to protect its rain forests and needs help from the international community to do the job. "We can't do it by ourselves," he said.

Guatemala's poorly equipped corps of forest rangers is being overwhelmed by powerful loggers and ranchers who operate in the vast El Petén rain forest, near its porous borders with Mexico and Belize. The Guatemalan army, itself the target of whispered corruption charges, provides only reluctant cooperation with the forest rangers. And in a country afflicted with guerrillas, drug traffickers, massive human rights violations and political chaos, rain forest protection does not appear to enjoy a high priority on the de León government's agenda.

In Honduras, the army is increasingly involved in rain forest protection, an activity the commanding general declares is nothing less than war. But the agency in charge of rain forest management is widely perceived as making its decisions for political reasons, and is scorned by many citizens. Massive deforestation along the Atlantic coast of Honduras led to mudslides and flooding that killed more than 200 people during a storm late in October.

"I AM THE CANCER"

Seated under a tree on a sweltering day in the Guatemalan rain forest hamlet of San Miguel, Reinaldo Gómez, 32, said he had probably deforested more than 100 acres in the Petén region since moving there a few years ago from the province of Alta Verapaz.

Fully aware of the damage he has wrought, Gómez shrugged and said: "I am the cancer of the rain forest."

Gómez, a father of three, grows corn and beans on a small plot in the forest, which provides for the basic food needs of his family. The only money he can earn—an average of $80 a month—is from cutting down mahogany trees.

"I know that every time I remove one of the trees, it increases the chances of deforestation," Gómez said. "But what am I to do? There is no other work here that pays anything."

In Honduras, José Atunez, 42, uses the same argument to justify hacking off the limbs of trees inside the Pico Bonito National Park rain forest, near the Caribbean port city of La Ceiba. Atunez scorches the removed limbs and then sells them for charcoal, which is widely used for cooking.

"Of course, it is not good to chop the rain forest's living wood, but sometimes, one is obligated to do so," said Atunez, a father of seven, pointing to a cluster of small children playing outside the family's one-room shack.

About 80 miles east of the national park, near the village of Tocoa, Alejandro Hernández and his brother, Francisco, had forded two streams and then hiked up winding, slippery mule trails to reach a plateau near the summit of a mountain, where they had located a 60-foot-tall mahogany tree.

The brothers would remain on the peak for a week—first sawing down the tree and then rolling it to a scaffold they had built nearby. There, with Alejandro standing atop the timber and Francisco below, and each grasping a handle at opposite ends of a 72-tooth saw, the brothers would begin the exhausting task of slicing the wood so it could be placed aboard a pair of mules and carried to the village, and from there trucked over a rutted, unpaved road to a loggers' cooperative in La Ceiba.

The brothers had come to the rain forest several years ago from the town of Santa Rosa, near the Guatemalan border, where they were earning about $3 a day as farm workers. Now, said Alejandro, a father of two (his brother has four children), harvesting mahogany enables each of them to earn about $10 a day, but life is not much easier, mostly because the wood is becoming scarcer and the brothers must climb farther and higher into the mountains to find suitable trees.

But there is no other alternative, Alejandro said.

"What else are we to do?" he asked.

Across the globe in the Philippines, the worst deforestation in Asia has led to catastrophic floods and mudslides. In December, floodwaters swept 24 people to their death on Leyte, the same island where 6,000 people were killed by a flood two years ago. Both floods were blamed on denuded hillsides, the result of rampant logging.

Very little forest cover is left in the country that was once the world's largest exporter of lumber and gave its name to a valuable species of hardwood known as Philippine mahogany.

Still, there is almost no national consensus in the Philippines about what needs to be done to rescue the rain forests or how to do it. Most everyone involved ducks responsibility. Environmentalists charge military personnel are often behind illegal logging. Overworked and underpaid forest rangers are often threatened by logging interests; some rangers have been murdered.

In nearby Malaysia, some of the world's most intensive logging of tropical hardwood continues unabated, despite promising experiments in rain forest management. That country's leader, Prime Minister Mahathir Mohamad, has consistently snubbed international calls for an end to logging and chastised the developed countries for preaching to the Third World.

JOBS, NOT BOYCOTTS

In an effort to save the rain forests, some environmental groups urge a consumer boycott of all mahogany furniture and ply-wood made from the *lauan*, or Philippine mahogany tree. Other rain forest advocates want consumers to buy only mahogany that has been certified as coming from areas with an internationally approved conservation plan.

But Rafael Leonardo Callejas, whose five-year term as president of Honduras ended Thursday, argues that the only way to preserve the rain forests is through the creation of jobs that would stanch the migratory movement into the forestlands.

"Destruction of the rain forests can only be stopped by the generation of jobs, which is what we don't have," Callejas said in an interview late in his presidency. "How can we tell a peasant not to chop down a mahogany tree if we don't have an alternative to offer him?"

In other words, the destruction of rain forests is in large part an economic problem that demands economic solutions.

Callejas advised environmentalists to lobby the U.S. Congress for wider access to the American market for a variety of Honduran and Guatemalan products, and thus help create jobs that would reduce population pressure on the Central American rain forests.

And that pressure builds daily in much of Latin America and Asia, where the relentless population shift from rural to urban areas is well documented. Less studied is the tidal wave of migration that brings more and more people streaming toward rain forests in search of land, crops—and mahogany.

> "Deforestation is a legitimate concern. However, the problem should be viewed objectively, not sensationally."

THE EXTENT OF RAIN FOREST DESTRUCTION HAS BEEN EXAGGERATED

Michael Sanera and Jane S. Shaw

Many commentators insist that environmentalists, the media, and the education system have overstated the extent of rain forest deforestation. Among these critics are Michael Sanera and Jane S. Shaw, who argue in the following viewpoint that educational textbooks grossly exaggerate the effects of rain forest cutting. These books overestimate the amount of rain forest area cut annually, Sanera and Shaw assert, without acknowledging the amount of land devoted to newly planted trees. The authors contend that school textbooks also exaggerate the threat of carbon dioxide buildup and the extent of species extinction due to rain forest deforestation. Sanera and Shaw are the authors of *Facts, Not Fear: A Parent's Guide to Teaching Children About the Environment*, from which this viewpoint is excerpted.

As you read, consider the following questions:

1. According to Sanera and Shaw, what do UN Food and Agriculture Organization figures on rain forest clearing actually include?
2. What are "debt-for-nature" swaps, according to the authors?
3. Why do Sanera and Shaw contend that it is inaccurate to call rain forests the "lungs of the earth"?

Around the globe at the equator lies a hot, humid, tropical belt of land, much of it covered by canopies of leafy trees. The understory teems with rich vegetation, exotic birds, a myriad of small mammals, and a multitude of insects.

This is the rain forest. And just about every schoolchild learns that it is in danger.

• An area the "size of the state of Nebraska is stripped of trees every year," says the Silver Burdett & Ginn text *World Geography: People in Time and Place*.

• One hundred acres of rain forest are destroyed every minute, says *50 Simple Things Kids Can Do to Save the Earth*. This is "enough to fill 50 football fields."

• "Some experts predict that if present practices continue, one-third of the world's tropical forests will vanish by the year 2000," says Scott Foresman's *History and Life*. "Other experts believe that all of the world's tropical rain forests could be gone by the turn of the century unless the deforestation is halted."

It isn't just that forests are being converted to cropland, these books say. The soil is soon exhausted since its nutrients have been absorbed by the trees and other vegetation. "Thus, within a few years, land once covered by awe-inspiring forest is reduced to useless wasteland," sums up Prentice Hall's *World Geography*.

North Americans are partly responsible for this devastation, the books say.

• "You can help save rain forests by not buying rain-forest woods such as teak and mahogany," says *Environmental Science*.

• Cattle ranches are replacing the rain forest, says *The Kids' Environment Book*. "Remember, the next Big Mac you eat may have started life as a cow in Brazil," it says.

• "Do you think a boycott of fast-food companies would halt the destruction of rain forests?" asks *Focus on Life Science*. "Would you be willing to participate in such a boycott?"

A MORE OBJECTIVE LOOK

Deforestation usually refers to the complete conversion of forest to cropland or other uses. Sometimes the wood from the forest is logged; at other times, trees are burned to clear the land.

Deforestation is a legitimate concern. However, the problem should be viewed objectively, not sensationally. One textbook, *Environmental Science: A Framework for Decision Making*, indicates that there are differences of opinion about the severity of the problem and includes an essay arguing that the extent of deforestation is exaggerated. But most textbooks tell only the scary part of the story.

Some conversion of the rain forest is not a bad thing. The United States experienced extensive forest clearing in the late nineteenth century. Many prominent people, including President Teddy Roosevelt, feared a "timber famine." They thought that the nation would run out of wood. But the "timber famine" never materialized. As prices rose, demand for wood declined, and supply increased. In addition, public and private efforts combined to encourage better forest management.

WORLD TROPICAL FOREST DATA

	Tropical Forests (all forest types)		Rain Forests			Tree Planting (all forest types)	
	Total Forest as % of Land Area	Deforesta-tion (annual)	Rain forest as % of Total Forest	Rain forest Deforesta-tion (annual)	Ratio of Total Forest /Rain forest Deforesta-tion* (in acres)	Tree Plant-ing as % of Total Forest	Ratio of Deforesta-tion/Tree Planting** (in acres)
Africa	24%	0.7%	16%	0.54%	184/1	.57%	32/1
Asia & Pacific	35%	1.2%	57%	1.2%	82/1	10.0%	2/1
Latin America & Caribbean	56%	0.8%	49%	0.42%	234/1	.94%	12/1
Total	37%	0.8%	41%	0.63%	158/1	2.5%	6/1

Source: United Nations, Forest Resources Assessment 1990, Tropical Countries #112, Food and Agriculture Organization of the United Nations, Tables 3, 4, 7, 8.

*For example, in Africa, for every 184 acres of rain forest, 1 acre was cut.

** For example, in Africa, for every 32 acres cut, one acre of new trees was planted.

"It is clear," say resource economists Roger A. Sedjo and Marion Clawson, "that dynamic growing societies will generate pressures on and changes in the forest resource base." The widespread clearing of tropical forests is likely to be temporary.

The textbooks are somewhat misleading about the estimates of rain forest clearing. Sedjo and Clawson, relying on numbers provided by the Food and Agriculture Organization of the United Nations, report that during the 1980s about 59,459 square miles of forest were cleared per year. This is about 0.8 percent of the tropical forest, and is in line with the many textbook estimates.

But these figures include *all types* of forests and vegetation in tropical areas, not just tropical rain forests. Children aren't told that tropical areas have six vegetation zones: tropical rain forests, moist deciduous forests, dry deciduous forests, very dry forests, desert zones, and hill and low-mountain zones. As the table above indicates, tropical rain forests are less than half the total forest in every area except Asia.

• So when books claim that "100 acres a minute" of rain forests are being destroyed, the actual figure is more like 21 acres a minute.

• When they say that rain forests the size of Nebraska are being destroyed every year, the actual number is about one-fourth that area or less than the combined areas of Vermont and New Hampshire.

Texts also mislead students by an almost complete failure to discuss the planting of new trees. In Asia, 10 percent of the total forest area is in forest plantations, and one acre of trees is planted for every two that are cut. In Latin America, even though tree plantations represent less than 1 percent of total forest area, about one-third of Latin America's output of wood for industrial use comes from them. The table above gives a more complete picture. . . .

SOME GOOD NEWS

Some positive developments have occurred that should make children feel better about the future of rain forests around the world. They include:

• Timber volume in the temperate climates (that is, not the tropics) is increasing rapidly, including in the former Soviet Union and Canada. In the United States, more timber is grown each year than is cut. The world is not running out of wood or trees.

• Wood production in Latin America is undergoing a major transition, say Sedjo and Clawson. Trees are being grown as crops in tree farms or plantations, where trees that are cut are continually replaced by new plantings.

• Detrimental policies of governments and the World Bank are beginning to change, and private conservation organizations around the world are taking action to protect the rain forest. For example, they have worked with the governments of countries that have rain forests to create "debt-for-nature" swaps.

"DEBT-FOR-NATURE" SWAPS

"Debt-for-nature" swaps are ways that private individuals around the world can help protect the rain forest or other areas of environmental concern. They emerged some years ago to give governments an incentive to protect resources

Many countries in the tropics engaged in heavy borrowing, especially during the 1970s, and are having trouble paying back these debts. Private environmental organizations like the Nature Conservancy and the World Wildlife Fund raise funds and then offer to pay a portion of a country's debts to other governments or banks.

If they pay off a bond owed by the government, for example, they receive in return the right to the interest that the government pays on the bond. This interest can be used to protect an environmental resource. Twenty-one debt-for-nature swaps had been made by the end of 1991, most of them in Costa Rica and Ecuador.

No one knows how significant swaps will be. Economists Robert T. Deacon and Paul Murphy point out that they represent a small amount of money (about $100 million) compared to the total debt of these countries. Also, there is no way to make governments carry out their part of the agreement if they don't wish to. But such swaps do provide an avenue for protection of the rain forest that wasn't there before. One swap between the World Wildlife Fund and Ecuador created a conservation fund that was twice as large as the government's budget for parks.

In the years ahead, we may see other innovative ideas as concerned people around the world offer funds for protection of special places. If preserving the rain forest is important to people in the rest of the world, it seems fair for them to help do it.

"Lungs of the Earth"?

When forests are cleared by burning, the fires release huge quantities of carbon dioxide into the air. Textbooks claim that this will increase global warming. And once the trees are cut down, they can no longer produce oxygen and absorb carbon dioxide through photosynthesis.

• "Destruction of vegetation reduces photosynthesis, and carbon dioxide levels in the atmosphere may increase," says *Biology Today*. "Some scientists predict this may contribute to a greenhouse effect—a global warming of the Earth's surface."

• The Scott Foresman text *History and Life* says that the rain forests "currently produce about 40 percent of all the oxygen that we breathe." If they are destroyed, carbon dioxide will build up in the atmosphere.

• *The Kids' Environment Book: What's Awry and Why* states that between 1 billion and 2.5 billion tons of carbon dioxide are added to the air every year as a result of deforestation. This is between one-fourth and one-half of all carbon dioxide released annually worldwide.

It is true that burning trees adds carbon dioxide to the atmosphere. Burning releases carbon from the trees, which then combines with oxygen to form carbon dioxide. In 1989 Richard A. Houghton and George M. Woodwell estimated that deforestation could add between 0.4 and 2.5 billion tons of carbon each year (in the form of carbon dioxide) to the air. But these are guesses with a wide range of uncertainty, and they pale in comparison to the 100 billion tons that Houghton and Woodwell say are emitted by plants and soil through a process called respiration.

Calling rain forests the "lungs of the earth," as curriculum material published by Zaner-Bloser does, or saying that the rain forests produce 40 percent of the world's oxygen implies that clearing the forests will affect our ability to breathe. And children take this message literally. Children have been known to make gasping sounds when they see paper littering the road—they have the idea that paper, which comes from trees, is taking oxygen out of the air.

Trees do contribute oxygen to the atmosphere through photosynthesis, but their contribution represents only a small part of the total amount of oxygen in the air. (Oxygen represents slightly more than 20 percent of our atmosphere.)

And while burning does add carbon dioxide, logging itself does not. (Some carbon dioxide is released from the soil after logging, however.) When trees are made into wood and used for construction of houses, their carbon is retained as long as the logs remain. The textbooks do not make this point.

SPECIES—EXTINCT BEFORE THEY ARE COUNTED?

Children are told that thousands of plant and animal species will become extinct due to the loss of the rain forests.

• "Scientists estimate that no fewer than one out of every two species on our planet dwells in the rain forest," says Prentice Hall's *World Geography.* "Many of these species have yet to be discovered. It is also estimated that one species of plant or animal life becomes extinct every day due to the cutting and burning."

• "Scientists estimate that over 100 species of plants in these forests are becoming extinct each day," reports Merrill's *Biology: An Everyday Experience.*

• Life-saving medicines will be lost. Linda Schwartz's book *Earth Book for Kids: Activities to Help Heal the Environment* says that the rain forests have plants that are used in 25 percent of all drugs and 70 percent of drugs used in cancer treatments.

It is true that many medicines, perhaps one-fourth of all prescription drugs, are derived from rain forest plants. But once the drugs have been identified, they can usually be made synthetically.

And it is possible that some important genetic material could be lost if species disappear with the rain forest. Some steps are being taken to protect these resources. Drug companies recognize that the tropics may contain the raw material for future drugs.

In 1991, Merck & Co. arranged to pay $1 million to the Instituto Nacional de Biodiversidad (INBio), a conservation and science group in Costa Rica that is trying to identify and catalog the country's plants, insects, and microorganisms. In return, Merck received exclusive rights to review samples from INBio for possible commercial applications for two years.

In spite of many claims, no one actually knows how many species are being lost in the rain forests or elsewhere in the world.

PERIODICAL BIBLIOGRAPHY

The following articles have been selected to supplement the diverse views presented in this chapter. Addresses are provided for periodicals not indexed in the *Readers' Guide to Periodical Literature*, the *Alternative Press Index*, the *Social Sciences Index*, or the *Index to Legal Periodicals and Books*.

Ronald Bailey	"Seven Doomsday Myths About the Environment," *Futurist*, January/February 1995.
Chris Brazier	"State of the World Report," *New Internationalist*, January/February 1997. Available from 1011 Bloor St. West, Toronto, ON M6H 1M1, Canada.
Gregg Easterbrook	"The Good Earth Looks Better," *New York Times*, April 21, 1995.
Malcolm Gillis	"Tropical Deforestation," *Vital Speeches of the Day*, April 1, 1996.
Gordon H. Orians	"Thought for the Morrow: Cumulative Threats to the Environment," *Environment*, September 1995.
Ed Regis	"The Environment Is Going to Hell and Human Life Is Doomed to Only Get Worse, Right? Wrong. Conventional Wisdom, Please Meet Julian Simon, the Doomslayer," *Wired*, February 1997. Available from PO Box 77265, San Francisco, CA 94107-0265.
Michael Sanera and Jane S. Shaw	"The ABCs of Environmental Myths," *Wall Street Journal*, September 4, 1996.
Karen Schmidt	"Life on the Brink," *Earth*, April 1997.
Julian L. Simon	"Doing Fine on Planet Earth," *Washington Times*, April 21, 1995. Available from Reprints, 3600 New York Ave. NE, Washington, DC 20002.
World & I	Special section on the global commons, April 1997. Available from 3600 New York Ave. NE, Washington, DC 20002.

CHAPTER 2

WHAT AGRICULTURAL POLICIES SHOULD BE PURSUED?

CHAPTER PREFACE

In November 1996, the United Nations convened the first World Food Summit to address the future food demands of a rapidly growing human population. At the meeting in Rome, participants discussed whether two of the world's forms of agriculture—the "Green Revolution" and sustainable agriculture—have the potential to feed approximately 100 million additional people per year, particularly in populous Third World nations.

The Green Revolution, a modern, high technology approach begun in the 1960s, incorporates the use of chemical fertilizers, pesticides, growth hormones, and genetically manipulated seed varieties. Credited with boosting food production in the Third World, "the revolution has nearly tripled world food output and boosted per-capita calories in the Third World by one-third," writes Hudson Institute researcher Dennis T. Avery. According to writers David Rothbard and Craig Rucker, "Modern agriculture, coupled with new technologies such as food irradiation and the seemingly unlimited prospects of biotechnology, could feed more than 10 times the number of people currently alive with not very much more land than is now in use."

However, many critics contend that Green Revolution food production has slowed, seemingly "reaching a plateau," according to Timothy Wirth, the U.S. undersecretary of state for global affairs. Environmentalists maintain that high-tech agriculture depletes resources such as nutrients, organic matter, and water and harms the environment through the use of chemicals. A more viable and efficient approach to meet food demands in the twenty-first century, these experts argue, is sustainable agriculture, which incorporates natural farming methods such as crop rotation, natural pest controls, and the use of organic fertilizers rather than chemicals and biotechnology. In the words of Jules N. Pretty, a sustainable agriculture program director, "Any investment in approaches that help the transition to sustainable agriculture is an investment both in the current and future capacity to feed the world."

Experts disagree whether Green Revolution production gains can be repeated in the twenty-first century and whether sustainable agriculture can produce similar results. The authors in the following chapter debate what agricultural policies should be pursued worldwide.

| "[The] shift away from chemical inputs is welcome environmental news."

ORGANIC FARMING OFFERS MANY BENEFITS

Gary Gardner

Organic farming involves the use of few or no chemicals or pesticides to grow crops. In the following viewpoint, Gary Gardner maintains that increasing numbers of farmers worldwide are adopting organic farming methods. Gardner argues that such reductions in the use of chemical fertilizers and pesticides, which he says contribute to water and soil pollution, benefit the environment. Gardner is a research associate for the Worldwatch Institute, a Washington, D.C., organization that studies environmental and other global problems.

As you read, consider the following questions:

1. What percentage of U.S. consumers purchase organic produce at least once per week, according to Gardner?
2. In Gardner's opinion, why are many farmers hesitant to adopt organic farming methods?
3. According to the author, what factor limits the expansion of organic agriculture?

From Gary Gardner, "Organic Farming Up Sharply," in *Vital Signs 1996: The Trends That Are Shaping Our Future* by Lester R. Brown, Christopher Flavin, and Hal Kane. Copyright ©1996 by Worldwatch Institute. Reprinted by permission of W. W. Norton & Company, Inc.

Output from organic farming is up sharply in the 1990s, with organic agriculture now regarded as a high-growth industry in some countries. Although global data are unavailable, several national and regional indicators reveal clear trends: organically cultivated area in the European Union expanded fourfold between 1987 and 1993, while the number of farmers in organic production doubled. In the United States, sales of organic farm products more than doubled between 1990 and 1994.

Although organic food captures only a small share of the total food market in most industrial countries—typically 2 percent or less—the half-decade of solid growth indicates that interest is more than fleeting. This stands in contrast to previous spurts in these sales, which were prompted by passing concerns about food safety.

What "Organic" Means

The definition of "organic" varies from country to country, and even within nations, but most definitions focus on highly restricted use of chemical fertilizers and pesticides. Because agriculture is a prime source of water and soil pollution in many countries, this shift away from chemical inputs is welcome environmental news.

The label "organic" is now applied to a variety of products beyond fresh produce, including personal care items and materials such as cotton. In the United States, land planted to organically grown cotton skyrocketed from just over 60 hectares in 1990 to more than 13,000 hectares certified or pending certification in 1994. The achievement is especially impressive given that cotton typically receives heavy pesticide treatments, accounting for some 25 percent of world insecticide use.

The Spread of Organic Farming

The blossoming of organic agriculture has several roots. Consumer demand for healthy food and increased awareness overall of agriculture's toll on the environment have driven much of the increase. A study by the Food Marketing Institute in the United States reports that 24 percent of U.S. shoppers purchase some natural or organic produce at least once a week. Such high demand has brought organics into mainstream supermarkets: 42 percent of U.S. supermarkets now carry some organic produce; these outlets posted a 23-percent rise in such sales in 1994. In Japan, where an estimated 3–5 million consumers buy organic produce regularly, demand for organics was the primary source of an 80-percent increase in U.S. exports of organic produce in 1994.

Latin American producers increasingly view organic production as an entree to lucrative niche markets. Mexico, for example, is now the world's largest producer of organic coffee, with thousands of certified growers. Aztec Harvests, an organic Mexican coffee, is marketed by peasant organizations directly to big-name clients such as United Airlines and Ben and Jerry's ice cream in the United States. Organic sesame, beans, bananas, vanilla, and vegetables are also being exported by peasant organizations in Mexico.

SALES OF ORGANIC FARM PRODUCTS IN THE UNITED STATES, 1980–94

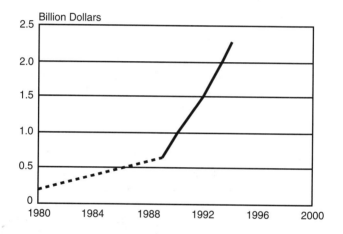

Source: Ken Mergentime, *In Business*, July/August 1995.

Some producers see organic production as a way to reduce farming costs. In India, the Karnataka Farmers Association, representing a third of the state's 30 million farmers, has formed an International Institute for Sustainable Agriculture to help increase farmer incomes by weaning them from dependence on expensive chemicals. In the United States, economic pressures, coupled with rising demand for organics, have prompted several corporations to switch to organic production: Fetzer and Gallo vineyards in California now use primarily organically produced grapes, and the Patagonia clothing company has pledged to switch to all-organic cotton in its 1996 product line.

In Germany, government subsidies for conversion to organic farming have boosted production. In an effort to reduce the environmental impact of farming and to meet consumer demand for healthier food, the government paid farmers 300–500 deutsche marks ($190–316) per hectare between 1989 and 1992 if they converted to organic farming. The subsidies help farmers through the risky transition period, when yields are suppressed as soils "withdraw" from dependence on chemical fertilizers and when organic produce cannot command a premium because certification is pending. Organic farms increased sixfold, and their area tenfold, throughout reunited Germany as a result of the subsidies.

Without support, many farmers are hesitant to risk the shift to organic production: a survey of Danish farmers revealed that one in five would like to switch, but find the prospect difficult and financially risky. The survey results prompted the government to devise an action plan to help farmers make the transition.

MAKING ORGANIC PRODUCE COMPETITIVE

Organic produce is often more expensive than conventionally grown food. In Germany, organics are typically priced 20–100 percent higher than conventional produce, in part because of a lack of competition at all levels of the processing chain. Higher labor costs and lower yields also contribute to the price difference, but these are not insurmountable obstacles. Scientists at the Rodale Institute in the United States note that most agricultural research has focused for decades on conventional agriculture; little attention was given to organic production. More research and greater competition could make organic produce competitive with conventionally grown foods.

The cost of organic produce and risks to organic farmers are both lessened in Japan through an innovative system known as teikei. Under this system, consumers—whether individually or as members of a cooperative—negotiate directly with farmers for delivery of organic produce during the growing season. The arrangement gives the organic farmer a guaranteed market for his or her goods, and provides consumers with organic produce at prices below those found in retail outlets. More than 1 million Japanese households participated in the teikei system in 1990 (before the current surge in organic production, which began in Japan in 1993). A similar system of production and distribution, known as community sustainable agriculture, is used in the United States.

Expansion of organic agriculture is limited, however, by the availability of organic nutrients at the farm level. Most urban organic waste is not returned to the farm; even if it were, one study noted that urban organic waste in the United States could meet only 10 percent of agricultural demand for nutrients. As a consequence, chemical fertilizers, which are shunned by organic farmers, are necessary for viable farming on a national scale.

Nevertheless, strong growth in organic agriculture is expected to continue. One analyst in Germany expects organic food's share of the market there to increase from 1.3 percent in 1993 to 8 percent by 2000. In the United States, federal standards for organic agriculture—along with a government seal for its products—are set to be issued, which is expected to boost both confidence and sales. Such trends are hopeful signs of a decreased dependence on polluting and unhealthy agricultural inputs.

| "On any broad basis, organic farming is unsustainable."

ORGANIC FARMING IS UNSUCCESSFUL

Dennis T. Avery

In the following viewpoint, Dennis T. Avery argues that organic farming is less efficient and more environmentally destructive than "high-yield" farming, in which chemical fertilizers and insecticides are used. Because it produces low crop yields, according to Avery, organic farming increasingly requires the conversion of large amounts of wildlife habitat to farmland, thereby resulting in environmental degradation. In addition, he maintains, organic farming cannot meet the food demands of the world's increasing population. Avery, a former U.S. Department of State senior agricultural analyst, is a senior fellow at the Hudson Institute, a public policy research organization in Indianapolis, and is the director of the institute's Center for Global Food Issues.

As you read, consider the following questions:

1. What would be the result of a "global attempt to rely on organic farming," in Avery's opinion?
2. According to Avery, what is organic farming's primary shortcoming?
3. What does the author mean by the "radical middle ground"?

Excerpted from Dennis T. Avery, *Saving the Planet with Pesticides and Plastics* (Indianapolis: Hudson Institute, 1995). Copyright ©1995 by Hudson Institute, Inc. Reprinted by permission of the author and publisher.

The secret is out. On any broad basis, organic farming is un-sustainable.

Environmental activists have focused worldwide discussion on the issue of "sustainable" food production. They have charged that high-yield farming's high-powered seeds are more suscepti-ble to pests than the traditional "landrace" varieties; that irriga-tion water supplies are running out; that soil erosion is stealing fertility from the fields; that pesticides cannot continue to cope with the insects and diseases; and that chemical-based farming will ruin soils and increase cancer rates among consumers.

None of these charges against high-yield farming is true. That's fortunate for the world, because organic farming offers no solution to the world's food or environmental problems.

Organic farming uses no manmade chemicals. It not only does without synthetic pesticides, but also foregoes manmade fertilizers. The organic producers believe that pesticides are dan-gerous to humans and the environment. They say manmade ni-trogen is bad for soils—though all nitrogen is elemental and chemically identical.

Organic farmers *do* use pesticides. They allow themselves the use of "natural" pesticides such as sulfur, a natural biopesticide called *Bacillus thuringiensis*, and pyrethrins (a chlorinated pest killer that is the natural product of a plant flower). Most or-ganic farmers spray more pesticide, more often, than non-organic farmers. . . .

DEGRADING THE ENVIRONMENT WITH ORGANIC FARMING

The day may come when we'll understand biology and ecology well enough at the level of cells and molecules to make organic farming a high-yield success. The new science of molecular bi-ology is beginning to peel away some of the layers of mystery now. But that in-depth knowledge is still at least decades away.

Until then, organic farming will produce far lower and far more erratic yields of many crops than science-based high-yield farming. Because of its lower yields, organic farming will thus force tillage of more crop acres to produce a given quan-tity of food.

With present knowledge levels, no responsible authority or organization should recommend either organic farming or tra-ditional low-yield farming systems as a broad-gauge alternative to high-yield agriculture. In fact, slashing farm chemical usage is likely to produce more soil erosion, more human cancer, and less wildlife habitat. At present, organic farming could not even sustain the fertility of our existing cropland, or protect it effectively from erosion.

Nor do the organic farming boosters offer any plan to feed the expanded world population of 2050. That alone makes it a nonstarter, because the rest of the world definitely plans to feed itself one way or another.

LOWER YIELDS ON ORGANIC FARMS

The yields of field crops from organic farming are only about half as high as those from mainstream high-yield farms—on a total-farm basis. Because of the low yields, any serious global attempt to rely on organic farming would force us to plow down millions of additional square miles of wildlife habitat for crops, legumes, and pasture.

Organic farmers and their advocates often claim to get "yields as good as their neighbors." In fact, the yields from an individual field of organically grown crops can be high—if productivity has been "borrowed" in the form of rotation with green manure crops (like clover) or spreading animal manure. I say "borrowing," because the high-yield organic acres are either lowering the cropping intensity or taking manure from feedlots or pasture acres. One famous "low-input" farm uses 18 tons of manure and municipal sludge per acre—plus some commercial fertilizer! . . .

ORGANIC FARMING NEEDS A CROP YIELD BREAKTHROUGH

If, as organic farming advocates sometimes claim, we could grow high yields of the crops the world demands without expensive off-farm inputs, all farmers would want to do it. They would save money and increase their profits. Presently, however, we cannot.

It makes little sense to applaud an organic farmer who gets county-average yields by importing huge amounts of animal manure and/or urban sewage sludge onto his acres. We already don't have enough organic nitrogen to go around.

If that organic farmer isn't doubling county-average yields, he isn't part of the wave of tomorrow, because the best mainstream farmers are doubling county averages. Or the new-wave organic farmer could be matching the county average with half the organic nitrogen. Otherwise, he's not part of the organic breakthrough we need.

Of course, organic farmers can make money. They get vastly higher prices. Their chemical costs are lower than those of mainstream farmers (even though, as mentioned above, they do use sprays, and quite a lot of them). However, their labor and management costs per acre are almost certainly higher, and often their labor constraints confine them to low production volumes.

But we're not worried here about organic farm incomes. The question is how to insure high and efficient yields per acre which can meet the needs of tomorrow and leave room for as much wildlife as we have today.

I freely concede that mainstream farmers have often used chemicals more heavily than was really necessary. They were encouraged in their prophylactic pesticide use by a poorly conceived set of government subsidies. That's not the key point either.

The key point is that mainstream farmers can safely step up their intensity and yields as the world needs it. Can organic farmers?

FAILING THE TEST

Organic agriculture does not pass the first test of sustainability: It cannot sustain the existing population of the world. Actions that undercut agronomy—the science of field-crop production—are detriments to the poor and to the environment. Such actions lead to the bringing of marginal lands into cultivation.

The sustainability of agricultural techniques is an important, valid concern, but such concerns do not legitimize technological and sociocultural regression.

Thomas R. DeGregori, Priorities, vol. 8, no. 4, 1996.

To be part of the solution, organic farmers need a productivity breakthrough. They need to produce more food with fewer natural resources and less erosion than organic farming would today produce if it was extended to the less ideal lands.

Our natural resources are scarce. We have alternative ways to get yields, but we have no alternative on wildlife.

Until now, organic farmers haven't thought yields were that important. To many organic producers, the important thing is how few chemicals they can use and still produce *something*. To many others, the size of the price premium they can get from frightened consumers is the key.

But the amount of land we use to produce food in the world governs how much land is left over from farming for forests, wildlife and other nonfarm uses. That's why minimizing the amount of land needed for crops is far more important to maintaining wildlife and the natural ecology than eliminating chemicals.

THE SHORTFALL IN ORGANIC PLANT NUTRIENTS

Low yields are only one disappointment about organic farming. Its biggest shortcoming is the global shortage of "natural" nitrogen fertilizer.

Experts at the U.S. Department of Agriculture have calculated that the available animal manure and sustainable biomass resources in the U.S. would provide only about one-third of the plant nutrients needed to support current food production.

Most of the world has far less pasture and manure per capita than the U.S. Globally, we may have less than 20 percent of the organic plant nutrients needed to sustain current food output. The only visible way to make up the shortfall would be to displace much more wildlife for legume crops.

There is no precise way to calculate the food shortfall or the wildlife encroachment which organic farming would force on the world, but it would be massive—hundreds of millions of tons of grain per year, and/or millions of square miles of wildlife.

This shortfall in plant nutrients should come as no great surprise. Organic farming deliberately does without the off-farm inputs used in most high-yield farming. Instead, organic farmers deliberately put a heavier burden on farming's "natural" resources. . . .

NEEDED: A RADICAL MIDDLE GROUND

For years, I've argued that neither organic farming nor chemically intensive farming as we've known it deserves to dominate our agriculture. Organic gives up too much productivity for a purism that can't be justified by any of the risks we can identify. High-chemical farming, for its part, has high production costs.

What we need is the *radical middle ground*, in which farmers use all of the most effective inputs they can get to get high yields at the lowest economic and environmental costs. What is reasonable? The lowest that will get the job done. How do we discover that? Through open competition, among systems, farms, and countries.

What we truly need is to abandon the old farm subsidies and international farm trade barriers. In America, the subsidies have tried and failed for 60 years to guarantee high net incomes for farmers. Eliminating the price supports and allotments would eliminate the artificial incentives for using chemicals.

Ending the farm trade barriers would also let American farms help provide the extra food that will be needed in an Asia nine times as densely populated as North America.

I think we would also see other benefits—more crop rotation, lower per-unit costs of production, and quite a lot less soil erosion. We might even see more family farmers than we get with price supports that encourage big, debt-leveraged one-man farms.

Free-market, low-cost, high-yield farming is the truly radical middle ground.

> "Intensive livestock agriculture is a substantial contributor to many environmental problems."

LIVESTOCK AGRICULTURE SHOULD BE ABOLISHED

Richard Schwartz

Livestock agriculture is the raising of such animals as cattle, poultry, and sheep for human consumption. In the following viewpoint, Richard Schwartz argues that animal agriculture contributes to numerous environmental problems and drains the world's natural resources. He contends that cattle ranching and production has been the chief cause of species endangerment and extinction in the United States and has contributed to the decline of wild animals on American lands. Furthermore, Schwartz maintains, livestock agriculture results in the generation of large amounts of greenhouse gases, the depletion of rain forests, the erosion and desertification of soil, and the consumption of large amounts of energy and water. Schwartz, author of *Judaism and Vegetarianism*, is a professor of mathematics at the College of Staten Island in New York.

As you read, consider the following questions:

1. According to Schwartz, how many acres of tropical forest are burned annually?
2. How much of America's water is used to raise livestock, according to Schwartz?
3. In the author's opinion, how many Americans each year are affected by chronic diseases resulting from animal-based diets?

From Richard Schwartz, "Abolishing Intensive Livestock Agriculture: A Global Imperative," *Animals' Agenda*, July/August 1996. Reprinted with permission from the *Animals' Agenda*, PO Box 25881, Baltimore, MD 21224.

Intensive livestock agriculture is a substantial contributor to many environmental problems. Livestock in the United States produce an incredible 230,000 pounds of manure per second, and much of it ends up in rivers, lakes, streams, and underground water sources. The amount of waste produced by 10,000 cattle in a feedlot equals that of a city of 110,000 people. In addition, huge amounts of chemical fertilizers and pesticides used in the production of animal feed crops end up in surface and ground waters.

ENVIRONMENTAL DEGRADATION

Current livestock agriculture contributes greatly to all four major global warming gases: carbon dioxide, methane, nitrous oxides, and chlorofluorocarbons. Every year millions of acres of tropical forest are burned, primarily to raise livestock, releasing millions of tons of carbon dioxide into the atmosphere. The highly mechanized agricultural sector uses a significant amount of fossil fuel energy, and this also contributes to carbon dioxide emissions. Cattle emit methane as part of their digestive and excretory processes, as do termites who feast on the charred remains of trees. The large amounts of petrochemical fertilizers used to produce feed crops for grain-fed animals create significant amounts of nitrous oxides. Also, the increased refrigeration necessary to prevent animal products from spoiling adds chlorofluorocarbons to the atmosphere.

Cattle ranching is a major cause of deforestation in Latin America. Since 1970, more than 25 percent of Central American forests have been destroyed in order to create pasture land for cattle. The production of just one quarter-pound hamburger imported from Mexico requires the clearing of 55 square feet of rain forest.

Livestock overgrazing causes erosion and the creation of deserts throughout the world. Cattle production is a prime component of the causes that lead to desertification: overcultivation of the land, improper irrigation techniques, and deforestation. According to the Worldwatch Institute, each pound of feedlot steak "costs" about 35 pounds of eroded American topsoil.

U.S. cattle production has resulted in significant biodiversity losses. According to the U.S. General Accounting Office, more plant species in the United States have been threatened or eliminated by livestock agriculture than by any other cause. The number of wild animals on the American range has dropped sharply, largely due to their inability to compete with cattle for food. Many species of plants and animals are disappearing annually because of the rapid destruction of rain forests.

Animal-based agriculture is also extremely wasteful of resources. A meat- and dairy-centered diet requires about 17 times as much land, 14 times as much water, and more than ten times as much energy as a completely plant-based diet.

Toles. Copyright 1992 The Buffalo News. Reprinted with permission of Universal Press Syndicate.

More than half the water consumed in the United States is used to raise livestock, primarily to irrigate land growing livestock feed. While a typical meat-eater's diet requires more than 4,000 gallons of water daily, a pure vegetarian's diet only uses 300 gallons. In California, the production of just one edible pound of beef uses 5,200 gallons of water, while only 23 gallons are needed to produce a pound of tomatoes. It takes about a hundred times more water to produce a pound of meat than it does to produce a pound of grain.

Another important resource issue today is energy, and livestock agriculture requires far more of it than does the production of vegetarian foods. The production of one pound of steak (500 calories of food energy) uses 20,000 calories of fossil fuels, most of which is used to produce feed crops. The annual beef consumption of a typical American family of four requires more than 260 gallons of fuel—as much as the average car uses in six months.

FOR A HEALTHIER DIET AND PLANET

When one considers the above facts, as well as the soaring health care costs associated with degenerative diseases caused by animal-based diets, it becomes increasingly clear that vegetarianism is not only an important individual choice, but also an imperative for national solvency and global survival. It is critical that people become aware of the far-reaching consequences of animal agriculture in order to shift away from a diet that is bankrupting the United States and the world, crippling and killing 1.5 million Americans annually with chronic diseases, threatening the world's ecosystems, wasting scarce resources, contributing to world hunger, and cruelly exploiting animals.

You can contribute to a more humane, peaceful, and healthy planet by further educating yourself on this issue. Such books as *Diet for a New America* by John Robbins (Stillpoint), *Beyond Beef* by Jeremy Rifkin (Dutton), and *Vegetarian Sourcebook* by Keith Akers (GP Putnam's) are excellent places to start. Enlighten others through personal conversations, meetings with opinion leaders in your community, letters and op-ed articles to newspapers and other publications, and calls to radio talk shows. There is a world to be saved, but global recovery is largely dependent on the demise of intensive animal agriculture. Within an individual's daily choice of diet lies the power to create a better world.

| "The optimum use of natural resources in the U.S. as well as other parts of the world involves use of both animals and plants to produce the nutrients humans require."

LIVESTOCK AGRICULTURE DOES NOT HARM THE ENVIRONMENT

National Cattlemen's Beef Association

The National Cattlemen's Beef Association (NCBA) is the marketing organization and trade association for America's one million cattle farmers and ranchers. In the following viewpoint, the NCBA argues that beef production does not degrade or exhaust such natural resources as land, water, energy, and grain. In addition, the NCBA maintains, livestock grazing is not a significant contributor to global warming and deforestation. The NCBA has offices in Chicago, Denver, and Washington, D.C.

As you read, consider the following questions:

1. What happens to cattle feedlot waste before its application to land as fertilizer, according to the NCBA?
2. According to the author, why is beef production often more energy efficient than plant food production?
3. What are the risks of a vegetarian diet, in the NCBA's opinion?

"How the Beef Industry Does Not Harm the Environment" by the National Cattlemen's Beef Association, March 1997. Reprinted by permission of the author.

A merican cattle producers are committed to protecting the environment and to the responsible use of natural resources. Cattlemen know it is in their best interest to maintain and improve the land and other resources because their livelihoods depend on it year after year. Cattle producers have chosen a way of life that allows them to be close to the land. They have a respect for the environment and the skills needed to manage resources, which are fostered by daily contact with the natural environment.

Western range conditions suffered early in the 1900s because of drought and overgrazing. Since then, livestock producers, range scientists and federal land managers have worked to improve conditions. The Society for Range Management found 79% of Bureau of Land Management lands, 86% of Forest Service lands and 86% of private lands to be stable to improving. Managed grazing results in better grass conditions than would exist if there were no grazing. Grazing is similar to mowing a lawn as it improves vegetation health and diversity.

WASTE MANAGEMENT

Manure production by all livestock and poultry is only a fraction of that claimed by critics, and it is fallacious to compare amounts of human and animal excrement. In the U.S. by far most human waste is immediately placed in water-borne sewage systems. Cattle feedlot waste, however, is deposited on soil or concrete surfaces where it undergoes a high degree of biodegradation before being applied to land for fertilizer purposes.

At least 60% of cattle manure, like that from wildlife, is deposited on the hundreds of millions of acres of pasture, open range and forest land, and it presents no pollution problem. In fact, animal droppings are important in maintaining water and mineral cycles on native rangeland.

The Environmental Protection Agency [EPA] says that "unconfined animal production is both environmentally sound and compatible with a high-quality environment," and that nitrogen and phosphorous levels in surface water from unconfined animal production are generally so low they are indistinguishable from background levels.

Management of feedlot surfaces, use of storage lagoons and holding ponds, and other management practices have helped prevent runoff and groundwater contamination problems. Essentially all beef cattle manure in feedlots is collected, loaded, hauled and applied as a natural fertilizer to soil directly or via storage/treatment systems. Tests show that groundwater quality in leading cattle feeding regions remains good. EPA data show that any water quality impairment of streams and rivers from all types of agricultural operations, including sediment from cropland, is less than 10% of the U.S. total of almost 1 million miles of streams.

METHANE PRODUCTION

Methane represents only 15% of the world's total greenhouse gases, and only 11% to 15% of world methane is attributable to cattle. Beef cattle in the U.S. account for only .5% of world methane production and only .1% of total greenhouse gases. Controlling methane emissions from cattle, even if it could be done, would provide little or no benefit from the point of view of global atmospheric chemistry and global warming. The major sources of methane are rice paddies, wetlands, biomass burning, fossil fuel exploration, landfills and coal mines.

LAND AND FOOD FOR CATTLE

In California, there is three times as much land that will not support crops as can be cropped. Much of this land can be grazed, however, and the soil erosion on most of the grazing land is as low—or lower—than on forests and "waste land."

In addition, cows eat things like citrus pulp, the dried grains left over from brewing, cottonseed (after the oil is crushed out), rice straw, and corn stover. These "food sources" contribute millions of tons of cattle feed that people are not going to eat.

Dennis T. Avery, *Saving the Planet with Pesticides and Plastic*, 1995.

If efforts were made to reduce cattle's methane production throughout the world, the best approach would be to follow production systems in the U.S. Modern technology, including products and programs to improve feed conversion, reduces methane production and improves animals' use of feed energy. In addition, U.S. cattle go to market at younger ages. All of this means that U.S. cattle contribute relatively much less to any possible global warming effect than do cattle in other countries.

DEFORESTATION

There is no evidence that shows livestock grazing has been a significant factor in deforestation of U.S. land. And there is little or no relationship between U.S. beef consumption and destruction of tropical rainforests. The U.S. imports no fresh beef from Brazil or other South American countries.

An examination of available information shows that conversion of forest to other uses, especially for grazing purposes, in the U.S. occurs much less frequently than claimed. A Department of Agriculture report showed that total U.S. forests declined by only 1% between 1977 and 1987. Most conversion was for recreational wildlife habitat, cropland, housing and developmental uses of land. At the same time, the amount of forest land converted for purposes of grazing actually declined during the same period.

Grazing is practiced on some deforested land in Latin America, but the primary causes of excessive rainforest destruction are not related to beef production. Most of the forestland conversion has been for crop and timber production, with grazing a residual use in some instances. Avoiding U.S. fast food hamburgers or other beef will do nothing to halt rainforest destruction. Imports represent only a small part of U.S. beef consumption. Only .6% of beef used in the U.S. comes from Central America or Brazil, and total fresh and frozen beef exports from Central America have declined 60% during the 1980s.

FOOD RESOURCES

The optimum use of natural resources in the U.S. as well as other parts of the world involves use of both animals and plants to produce the nutrients humans require. Cattle production does not prevent production of plant-source food for domestic and overseas use. The U.S. has more than enough cropland to grow both feed grains and food crops. In fact, because of grain surpluses, government crop programs involve removal of land from grain production.

The world hunger problem is a result of poverty, lack of buying power and food distribution problems—not eating meat in the U.S. The U.S. continues to produce more grain than can readily be sold. For most of the last three decades, U.S. grain surpluses have increased. However, the increase in grain supplies has not helped alleviate world hunger. If grain were not fed to livestock, more grain would not necessarily be available to feed the hungry. Relief programs and/or economic development in poor countries are needed.

THE ENVIRONMENTAL EFFICIENCY OF BEEF PRODUCTION

Beef cattle spend all or most of their lives on pasture and range. At least 83% of the nutrients consumed by cattle come from non-grain sources—feedstuffs not edible by humans. These feedstuffs include grass, roughage and crop aftermath. Livestock also consume 18 billion pounds (25%) of the by-products generated by food processing—products that would otherwise be wasted or be hauled to landfills and dumps.

The total amount of water used to produce and process a pound of boneless beef from the farm to the plate averages 441 gallons. For comparison, the amount of water used to produce similar portions of pork and poultry averages 385 gallons and 337 gallons, respectively. Mature cattle consume 8 to 15 gallons of water per day, depending on temperature, humidity and type of feed consumed. Most of this water returns to the soil. In total, beef cattle consume less than two-tenths of 1% of total water used annually in the U.S.

U.S. agricultural production accounts for 2.5% of total fossil fuel energy used in the U.S., and .5% is used for beef production. Eighty-two percent of the total fossil energy involved in food production, processing and preparation is used after food leaves the farm. Because many plant-source foods require large amounts of energy in the processing phase, the overall energy efficiency of beef often is comparable, or even superior, to the energy efficiency of plant-source foods.

DIET AND HEALTH

Excess fat, from any source, can contribute to the development of illness in some people. But beef and fat are not necessarily synonymous. Trimmed beef has long been part of diets which have contributed to improved health and continuing increases in the longevity of Americans. Lean beef is regarded by leading health organizations and agencies as a valuable and appropriate part of American diets. The American Dietetic Association, the American Heart Association, the National Heart, Lung and Blood Institute, and other organizations generally recommend 5 to 7 ounces of lean, trimmed meat daily. Nutrition authorities point out that trimmed beef provides large amounts of essential nutrients, such as iron, zinc, vitamin B-12 and balanced protein.

Just because a diet is lower in meat doesn't mean it's higher in health. A strictly vegetarian diet may lack essential nutrients a body needs. Scientists at Canada's National Institute of Nutrition, who compared vegetarian diets to diets that include meats, concluded that "insufficient data exist from well-controlled studies to support claims of unique health benefits of vegetarian diets." The analysis also showed that vegetarian diets place adults—especially pregnant and lactating women—at a higher risk for anemia, and children at higher risk for rickets and slower growth.

| "The new biotech fruits and
vegetables will present benefits both
to producers . . . and to consumers."

GENETICALLY ENGINEERED FOODS SHOULD BE PRODUCED

Susanne L. Huttner

In recent years, scientists have manipulated the genetic makeup of some plants in order to improve the quality of the foods they produce. In the following viewpoint, Susanne L. Huttner argues that numerous scientific reports have found no undue risks from the consumption of genetically engineered foods. She contends that genetically engineered foods offer both producers and consumers many benefits, including higher crop yields and more nutritious produce. Huttner is the director of the University of California's Systemwide Biotechnology Research and Education Program in Berkeley.

As you read, consider the following questions:

1. What are the two factors that affect the potential of agricultural biotechnology, according to Huttner?
2. In the author's opinion, how may consumers view foods labeled as "genetically engineered"?
3. According to Huttner, what should be the focus of regulation concerning food products?

From Susanne L. Huttner, "Getting the Products of Biotechnology to Market," Priorities, vol. 7, no. 3, 1995. Reprinted with permission from Priorities, a publication of the American Council on Science and Health, 1995 Broadway, 2nd Floor, New York, NY 10023-5860.

Agricultural biotechnology provides breeders and farmers with important new tools that can positively and significantly impact crop-production efficiency and value and provide consumers with a broad range of improved fruit and vegetable products. The tools of biotechnology are being used to control ripening and spoilage, allowing fruits and vegetables to reach the marketplace at the peak of ripeness and freshness. Biotechnology also adds new weapons to the farmers' arsenal by providing biological strategies to fight insects and plant disease. The tools of biotechnology are used to improve the nutrient composition, texture and flavor of both fresh and processed foods and to improve bacterial and yeast cultures used in bread, cheese and yogurt production. Biotechnology is, in fact, used in virtually every segment of today's food-production system.

ACHIEVING FULL POTENTIAL

Thanks to biotechnology, we can expect to see a number of new agricultural products by the year 2000. By 2005, as our knowledge of plant genetics grows, the kinds of improvements plant geneticists and breeders will achieve and the range of crops affected will expand rapidly.

The extent to which agricultural biotechnology achieves its fullest potential depends, in large part, on two important factors: government regulation and public acceptance. Government regulation can encourage innovation or—particularly in the case of government-mandated labeling—it can create disincentives to the adoption and use of new technologies. The degree of public acceptance likewise can create or diminish marketplace demand. Moreover, government regulation and perceptions of public acceptance are often interactive, creating the potential either for rapid progress or for a disastrous downward spiral.

NO DANGER

Many of us in the scientific community believe that the fundamental issues regarding the nature of the risks presented by the new genetic methods have largely been settled. At least a dozen national and international reports, issued by respected scientific and science-policy groups, agree that:

- The use of recombinant DNA [splicing together DNA fragments from different organisms, often from different species] does not, per se, introduce any new safety concerns when the new techniques are compared to conventional breeding methods.
- The new techniques are in many ways more selective and

reliable than conventional breeding methods.

- To the extent that we know more about the kinds of genetic changes being made, risk assessment is enhanced.

The consensus reached within the scientific community was expressed in the 1987 National Academy of Sciences report on the risks associated with field research which noted that:

- There is no evidence of the existence of unique hazards either in the use of recombinant DNA (rDNA) techniques or in the movement of genes between unrelated organisms.
- The risks associated with the introduction of rDNA-engineered organisms are the same in kind as those associated with the introduction of unmodified organisms and organisms modified by other methods.
- The assessment of risks associated with introducing rDNA organisms into the environment should be based on the nature of the organism and of the environment into which the organism is to be introduced, and independent of the method of engineering.

In an expanded report issued in 1989, the National Research Council agreed: "No conceptual distinction exists between genetic modification of plants and microorganisms by classical methods or by molecular techniques that modify DNA or transfer genes."

GENE SPLICING IMPROVES FOODS

The new "gene splicing" techniques are being used to achieve many of the same goals and improvements that plant breeders have sought through conventional methods—the techniques that bring us hybrid peas, and disease resistant wheat. Today's techniques are different from their predecessors. . . . They can be used with greater precision and allow for more complete characterization and, therefore, greater predictability about the qualities of the new variety.

David A. Kessler, *CQ Researcher*, August 5, 1994.

There exists wide scientific agreement that the use of genetic manipulation techniques in general, or the newest techniques—such as rDNA—in particular, do not warrant a new regulatory paradigm. Both theory and experience support this view, reflecting the fact that distinctions between genetic combinations that occur in nature and those that do not are, at base, very murky. Similarly, when comparing genetic changes achieved by older techniques with those brought about by newer techniques, how a change is achieved does not correlate with risk.

Moreover, there is vast experience—among plant breeders, geneticists, industry representatives, regulators and even consumers—with products derived from organisms with genetic combinations that are new or that never would exist in nature. Think of the broccoflower, the tangelo, the pumpkin and the other new fruit and vegetable varieties introduced into our markets each year.

Common sense dictates that the characteristics of a product—such as pathogenicity or toxigenicity—and the product's intended use determine the degree to which regulation is needed to safeguard public health or environmental quality. In considering new food products, the Food and Drug Administration (FDA) has applied—with greatest fidelity—principles of regulatory policy that are supported by the scientific consensus.

FEDERAL OVERSIGHT

A May 1992 policy statement clarifies that the FDA's regulation of new food varieties developed through modern genetic techniques will be the same as their regulation of all other foods. The level of oversight given to a new food will depend on that food's inherent characteristics, not on the method by which it was developed. The FDA's policy has been supported by the American Medical Association and the American Dietetic Association.

Under this policy, the FDA will not ordinarily require premarket review if the food constituents from a new plant variety are the same or substantially similar to substances currently found in other foods. Premarket approval will be required, however, when the characteristics of a new variety raise significant safety questions or when a new food is not considered substantially equivalent to existing foods.

Any food that contains a substance new to the food supply and that does not have a history of safe use will thus require premarket approval. Similarly, any food that contains increased levels of a natural toxicant will require approval and could be banned from the marketplace.

The policy also addresses the potential for introducing an allergen into a food in which a consumer would not expect it. Foods derived from known allergenic sources must be demonstrated not to be allergenic or must be labeled to identify the source. In cases posing potentially serious risk of allergenicity, such foods would be banned from the food supply.

Thus, there is broad agreement that where claims of unique or heightened food safety risk are considered by regulators, they are best judged within the context of our experience with similar foods produced by conventional techniques. Scientific consensus does not support regulatory schemes that set all or most new biotech foods apart for special reporting requirements or labeling.

LABELING

But not everyone has adhered to sound scientific principles when evaluating new biotech foods. Consumers Union, the organization behind *Consumer Reports* magazine, has requested that the FDA require labeling for all genetically engineered foods from plant varieties with traits not commonly found in the breeding line from which that variety was derived. As noted above, however, plant breeders, regulators and consumers all have had extensive experience with new fruit and vegetable varieties created by crossbreeding common crops with wild relatives that introduce traits never before expressed in those breeding lines.

Food safety is not a function of the "newness" of the genes and proteins introduced by breeding or genetic engineering. Nor is it a function of the genetic modification method; rDNA techniques do not change the fundamental biochemical rules of gene expression and protein synthesis.

Quite simply, there is no reason for treating new biotech foods differently from other, similar foods. Nonetheless, certain groups that are pressing for labeling of all or most genetically engineered foods hold that consumers have a right to make choices. Those against labeling foods as "genetically engineered" point out that such labels would provide consumers with no information on the kinds of changes made in the product.

Such labeling would present a serious disincentive to the processed-food industry, where product prices generally are low and highly competitive. The industry typically uses produce that is pooled from many sources before it is processed and canned. Labeling would require that genetically engineered fruits and vegetables be kept separate at all stages of production—at the farm, in shipping, in processing and in canning. That separate handling would mean added costs.

MANY BENEFITS

The new biotech fruits and vegetables will present benefits both to producers (yield, reduced spoilage, enhanced processing) and to consumers (taste, nutrition); but most of them will represent incremental, rather than sweeping, improvements over other varieties. The added production costs resulting from mandatory labeling very likely will not be offset by proportionately higher market prices for the new products. Moreover, consumers unfamiliar with genetic engineering may not view a label reading "genetically engineered" or "product of biotechnology" as indicating a clear benefit—they may, instead, view it as a warning.

Consider, for example, the processed tomato industry. Canned tomato products such as tomato sauce, tomato paste and catsup represent a $1.1 billion market. One market share—one percent of the market—equals more than $100 million. The industry has little incentive to use genetically engineered tomatoes in the face of government-mandated labeling given the resultant added production costs and possible loss of consumer acceptance.

If the new biotech foods are judged safe by accepted scientific criteria, it is unfair to subject them to this "risk-benefit trap" that moves forward only those new products that can garner high prices in the marketplace. To the academic researchers who are contributing to the development of new food products—with research supported by public funding—it is of particular concern that new biotech foods may not reach the greater part of the public but may end up being sequestered to the higher income markets.

The development and adoption of new agricultural biotechnology products has faced a complex web of issues and concerns. The scientific community views the debate over risk assessment and regulation as settled. The use of rDNA techniques and the behavior of rDNA-modified organisms has been extensively evaluated over the past two decades. We have more than a decade of experience worldwide with more than 1,000 carefully monitored field trials of rDNA-modified plants.

This experience confirms the view that regulation should focus on the new traits or modifications made in products, not on the genetic method used. In the matter of regulation, whether of field research or the introduction of new foods, government should impose only those burdens on research and commercial development that are commensurate with the risks indicated by those new traits or modifications.

Scientifically sound risk assumptions and regulations—like the FDA's food policy—that are crafted with sufficient flexibility to accommodate new knowledge as it is generated are the essential foundations for public policies that, on the one hand, safeguard public health and the environment and, on the other, promote innovation, economic competitiveness and the delivery of a wide array of new products to consumers.

> "Genetic engineering poses the greatest danger of any technology yet introduced."

GENETICALLY ENGINEERED FOODS ARE DANGEROUS

John B. Fagan

Genetically engineered foods are being produced and sold without regard for human health, and their many damaging effects will be irreversible, John B. Fagan argues in the following viewpoint. Fagan maintains that genetically engineered foods are inadequately tested and that genetic manipulation can produce unanticipated and harmful side effects, such as the introduction of dangerous allergens and toxins into foods that were previously safe. Fagan is a professor of molecular biology and chemistry at Maharishi University of Management in Fairfield, Iowa.

As you read, consider the following questions:
1. What is the assumption of the food industry and government concerning genetically engineered foods, according to Fagan?
2. According to Fagan, what is the origin of many weaknesses in plants, animals, and humans?
3. In the author's opinion, why will the health-damaging effects of genetic engineering be permanent?

From John B. Fagan, "Genetically Engineered Food: A Serious Health Risk," posted on the World Wide Web February 26, 1997, at http://www.natural-law.org/issues/genetics/gehazards.html. Reprinted by permission of the author.

Genetically engineered foods containing genes derived from bacteria and viruses are now starting to appear in the shops, and foods with insect, fish, and animal genes will soon follow. These genetic changes are radically different from those resulting from traditional methods of breeding. Yet, the sale of these foods is being permitted without proper assessment of the risks and without adequately informing the public, even though many scientists say that genetically modified foods could cause serious damage to health and the environment.

What is genetic engineering? Genes are the blueprints for every part of an organism. Genetic engineering is the process of artificially modifying these blueprints. By cutting and splicing DNA— genetic surgery—genetic engineers can transfer genes specific to one type of organism into any other organism on earth.

Why do it? Scientists want to transfer desirable qualities from one organism to another; for example, to make a crop resistant to an herbicide or to enhance food value.

Is it necessary? At first sight it may seem appealing. However, closer examination reveals that commercial and political motives are taking precedence with little regard to the possible dangers. We already have the ability to feed the world's population without the risks posed by genetic engineering. Why subject humanity to these unnecessary risks?

A VARIETY OF DANGERS

What are the dangers? (Please see more detailed discussion below.) Those identified so far include:

- New toxins and allergens in foods
- Other damaging effects on health caused by unnatural foods
- Increased use of chemicals on crops, resulting in increased contamination of our water supply and food
- The creation of herbicide-resistant weeds
- The spread of diseases across species barriers
- Loss of bio-diversity in crops
- The disturbance of ecological balance
- Artificially induced characteristics and inevitable side-effects will be passed on to all subsequent generations and to other related organisms. Once released, they can never be recalled or contained. The consequences of this are incalculable.

What is the situation now? Genetically modified foods available, or about to appear, in U.S. markets include tomatoes, squash, yeast, corn, potatoes, and soybeans (which are used in 60% of all processed foods, such as bread, pasta, candies, ice cream, pies, biscuits, margarine, meat products and vegetarian meat substitutes). Genetically modified organisms are also used to produce cheeses and canola oil. But this is just the beginning.

Scrumptious tomato with ten thousand year shelf life
FDA: no need to test or label this food

yummy crunchy celery with hammer protein
FDA: watch your thumb

succulent vegetable pig with pumpkin protein
FDA: be sure to cook pumpkin pie thoroughly

genetically engineered consumers who support FDA policy
FDA: you are what you eat

©1992 Mickey Siporin

©Mickey Siporin, Siporin Studios, Upper Montclair, NJ. Reprinted with permission.

The food industry and government appear to be complacent. They assume that these new foods are not substantially different from existing foods and pose no special risks. But this assumption is wrong and dangerous. The radical changes being made by biotechnologists could never happen in nature, and have already caused toxic side-effects. Current regulations require only minimal safety testing for some foods, and none at all for others. In no case do regulations require evaluation of long-term impacts on health. Most genetically modified foods will not be labelled. Under present regulations manufacturers are already introducing genetically modified ingredients into many processed foods without informing consumers. The government is ignoring the wishes of the public. Surveys consistently find that 85–90% of consumers want clear labelling of all genetically engineered foods.

Despite intended benefits, many technologies produce disastrous side-effects. Increasingly, society is recognizing side-effects such as nuclear pollution, global warming, and the toxic effects of pesticides and herbicides. Medicines are often withdrawn because the side-effects turn out to be too poisonous. In every case, it has taken time for hazards to come to light and for action to be taken.

Genetic engineering poses the greatest danger of any technology yet introduced. Because many of the damaging effects of genetic engineering are irreversible, we must prevent problems before they occur. The precautionary approach is essential if we are to protect ourselves, our children, and all generations to come. We must take action now, if we want to prevent an avalanche of genetically engineered foods from inundating the market and placing virtually everyone at risk.

We must act Before It Is Too Late! Genetically engineered foods are being introduced without due regard for health, yet many damaging effects will be irreversible.

WHAT IS NEEDED

To protect our health:

- Any food produced through genetic engineering should be banned until scientifically shown to be safe and safe for everyone.
- In the meantime, labelling should be required for any food that contains even one genetically engineered ingredient, or that has been produced using genetically modified organisms or enzymes.
- Full disclosure labelling will allow consumers to choose what they eat. It will also help scientists trace the source of health problems arising from these foods.

To protect the environment:

- All applications of genetic engineering should be banned that carry the risk of accidental or intentional release of genetically modified organisms into the environment.

What you can do:

- Write to members of Congress, food producers, supermarkets, the press and consumer groups, expressing your concern. . . .

DANGERS OF GENETICALLY ENGINEERED FOODS

The scientific facts demonstrating the need for an immediate worldwide ban. Because living organisms are highly complex, genetic engineers cannot possibly predict all of the effects of introducing new genes into them. This is the case for even the simplest bacterium, not to mention more complex plants and animals. This is because:

- the introduced gene may act differently when working within its new host
- the original genetic intelligence of the host will be disrupted
- the new combination of the host genes and the introduced gene will have unpredictable effects; and therefore
- there is no way of knowing the overall, long-term effect of genetically engineered foods on the health of those who eat them.

The following are some of the facts:

• *Unnatural gene transfers from one species to another are dangerous.* Biotechnology companies erroneously claim that their manipulations are similar to natural genetic changes or traditional breeding techniques. However, the cross-species transfers being made, such as between fish and tomatoes, or between other unrelated species, would not happen in nature and may create new toxins, diseases, and weaknesses. In this risky experiment, the general public is the guinea-pig.

• *Biotechnology companies also claim their methods are precise and sophisticated.* In fact, the process of inserting genes is quite random and can damage normal genes. Genetic research shows that many weaknesses in plants, animals, and humans have their origin in tiny imperfections in the genetic code. Therefore, the random damage resulting from gene insertion will inevitably result in side-effects and accidents. Scientists have assessed these risks to be substantial.

• *Unpredictable health damaging effects.* When genetic engineers insert a new gene into any organism there are "position effects" which can lead to unpredictable changes in the pattern of gene expression and genetic function. The protein product of the inserted gene may carry out unexpected reactions and produce potentially toxic products. There is also serious concern about the dangers of using genetically engineered viruses as delivery vehicles (vectors) in the generation of transgenic plants and animals. This could destabilize the genome, and also possibly create new viruses, and thus dangerous new diseases.

• *Genetically engineered products carry more risks than traditional foods.* The process of genetic engineering can thus introduce dangerous new allergens and toxins into foods that were previously naturally safe. Already, one genetically engineered soybean was found to cause serious allergic reactions, and bacteria genetically engineered to produce large amounts of the food supplement tryptophan have produced toxic contaminants that killed 37 people and permanently disabled 1,500 more.

- *Increased pollution of food and water supply.* More than 50% of the crops developed by biotechnology companies have been engineered to be resistant to herbicides. Use of herbicide-resistant crops will lead to a threefold increase in the use of herbicides, resulting in even greater pollution of our food and water with toxic agrochemicals.
- *Health-damaging effects caused by genetic engineering will continue forever.* Unlike chemical or nuclear contamination, genetic pollution is self-perpetuating. It can never be reversed or cleaned up; genetic mistakes will be passed on to all future generations of a species.
- *Inadequate government regulation.* Biotech companies claim that government regulatory bodies will protect consumers. However DDT, Thalidomide, L-tryptophan, etc. were approved by U.S. regulators with tragic results. Recently it was found that 80% of supermarket milk contained traces of either medicines, illegal antibiotics used on farms, or hormones, including genetically engineered bovine growth hormone (rbGH). The facts show that regulators are not protecting the public adequately.
- *Ethical concerns.* Transferring animal genes into plants raises important ethical issues for vegetarians and religious groups. It may also involve animal experiments which are unacceptable to many people.
- *Gene transfer across species and competition from new species damaging the environment.* When new genetic information is introduced into plants, bacteria, insects or other animals, it can easily be passed into related organisms, through processes such as cross pollination. This process has already created "super weeds." Existing species can also be displaced from the ecosystem with disastrous effects, as happened with genetically modified Klebsiella soil bacteria.
- *Crops are now being engineered to produce their own pesticides.* This will promote the more rapid appearance of resistant insects and lead to excessive destruction of useful insects and soil organisms, thus seriously perturbing the ecosystem. In addition, the pesticide produced by the plant may be harmful to the health of consumers.

GLOBAL THREAT TO HUMANITY'S FOOD SUPPLY

Giant transnational companies are carrying out a dangerous global experiment by attempting to introduce large numbers of genetically engineered foods widely into our food supply. Because genetic manipulations can generate unanticipated harmful side-effects, and because genetically engineered foods are not tested sufficiently to eliminate those that are dangerous, this experiment not only jeopardizes the health of individuals, but could also lead to national or even global food shortages and large-scale health threats. There is no logical scientific justification for exposing society to this risk, nor is it necessary to take this risk for the purpose of feeding humanity. It is only of benefit to the biotech industry, which will obtain short term commercial gains at the expense of the health and safety of the whole population. Tampering with the genetic code of food is reckless and poses a serious threat to life. It could easily upset the delicate balance between our physiology and the foods that we eat. There is already ample scientific justification for an immediate ban on genetically modified foods in order to safeguard our health.

PERIODICAL BIBLIOGRAPHY

The following articles have been selected to supplement the diverse views presented in this chapter. Addresses are provided for periodicals not indexed in the *Readers' Guide to Periodical Literature*, the *Alternative Press Index*, the *Social Sciences Index*, or the *Index to Legal Periodicals and Books*.

Ryan Andrews	"New Routes to Hardy Crops," *World & I*, June 1996. Available from 3600 New York Ave. NE, Washington, DC 20002.
David Evans	"Produce on Demand: What's Good for US Market is Good for World Markets, Too," *Nature Biotechnology*, July 1996. Available from PO Box 5054, Brentwood, TN 37024-5054.
Forum for Applied Research and Public Policy	Special section on desertification, Fall 1996. Available from Energy, Environment, and Resources Center, University of Tennessee, Knoxville, TN 37996-0710.
Gary Gardner	"Shrinking Fields: Cropland Loss in a World of Eight Billion," *Worldwatch Papers*, no. 131, July 1996. Available from 1776 Massachusetts Ave. NW, Washington, DC 20036.
Verlyn Klinkenborg	"Farming Revolution: Sustainable Agriculture," *National Geographic*, December 1995.
Susan Meeker-Lowry	"The War on Nature," *Toward Freedom*, November 1995.
Mark Ritchie	"The Right to Food," *Yes!* Winter 1997. Available from 157 Waterloo Rd., London SE1 8UU, England.
Mark W. Rosengrant and Robert Livernash	"More Food, Less Damage," *Environment*, September 1996.
Julian L. Simon	"What the Starvation Lobby Eschews...," *Wall Street Journal*, November 18, 1996.
Elroy Webster	"Farmers Are Putting the Environment First," *USA Today*, January 1997.
Timothy Wirth	"Ways to Fight Hunger," *Christian Science Monitor*, November 14, 1996. Available from Newspaper Indexing Center, Microphoto Division, Old Mansfield Rd., Wooster, OH 44691.

CHAPTER 3

WHAT ENERGY SOURCES SHOULD BE PURSUED?

CHAPTER PREFACE

Throughout history, humans have relied on energy from the sun. In ancient times, Greeks used mirrors to collect solar energy. Centuries later, in 1839, French scientist Edmund Becquerel discovered that sunlight shining on specific materials could cause a spark of electricity and, under certain conditions, form an electric current.

Since then, photovoltaic (PV) technology—in which silicon cells convert sunlight into electricity—has developed into a viable energy source. More than one hundred thousand U.S. homes, mostly in rural areas, exclusively use solar power. Utility companies in California, New York, Texas, and other states now install PV systems on residential rooftops. In other nations, primarily in the Third World, many homes that cannot be connected to utility grids because of high costs could eventually be powered by solar cells. Indeed, organizations such as the World Bank are investing tens of millions of dollars to equip Third World homes with PV systems. According to the Union of Concerned Scientists, of all forms of energy, "solar has the greatest potential for providing clean, safe, reliable power."

Despite such progress, high costs have prevented solar power from becoming as popular an energy source as proponents would like. In the words of photovoltaics researcher Eldon Boes, "The basic problem with the solar industry is simple: High-performance solar cells cost too much." Many observers argue that because electricity produced from coal-burning and nuclear power often costs several times less than solar-generated electricity, utility companies should continue relying on these cheaper sources rather than solar energy. According to writer Michael Fox, "To hold out the hope that [solar energy] will provide a large supply of bulk energy is really to mislead an uninformed public with promises that cannot be fulfilled."

Solar energy is just one of many sources of energy that could be exploited to meet global energy demands. The contributors in this chapter debate which of these energy sources should be pursued.

| "The 21st will be the century of the photon, including solar photons, from which humankind must once again learn to live."

THE USE OF SOLAR POWER SHOULD BE INCREASED

Gerd Eisenbeiss

Gerd Eisenbeiss is the program director of the German Aerospace Research Agency. In the following viewpoint, Eisenbeiss argues that because of the environmental threats posed by the burning of fossil fuels, reliance on solar power is an "ecological necessity." In addition, according to Eisenbeiss, the development of solar energy technology is made necessary by the inevitable depletion of Earth's energy resources. Eisenbeiss describes several types of solar power systems in America, Germany, and Spain that are producing energy. He concludes that with new technological improvements, solar power can become an increasingly efficient energy source.

As you read, consider the following questions:

1. How does Eisenbeiss compare solar energy and fossil fuels?
2. According to the author, where is approximately half of the world's solar electricity produced?
3. What are the pros and cons of the updraft power station, according to Eisenbeiss?

From Gerd Eisenbeiss, "Renewable Resources: Where Will Tomorrow's Energy Come From?" *Deutschland* magazine, October 1996. Copyright © Frankfurter Societäts-Druckerei GmbH. Reprinted courtesy of the publisher.

S olar energy has promoted the development of humankind and there would be no life on Earth without it. Even when human beings first tamed fire, it was plants—which had grown because of solar energy—that were burnt to provide warmth and light. It was only in the 19th century that they were joined by coal and oil. As a result of this, human beings began to use and extract the fossil energy deposits that had been accumulated over billions of years, and which were also formed by the sun. This fossil age, however, will remain only a brief period in the history of the Earth and humankind. Before this period there was—and there must someday be again—a solar civilization. This is the "solar logic" from which, in the long term, there is no escape.

The ecological necessity of using solar energy results first and foremost from the increasingly more evident threat to our climatic system caused by carbon dioxide as the end product of all the combustion processes involving carbon-based fuels. The build-up of this gas in our atmosphere triggers a sort of greenhouse effect which has led to a measurable warming, whose effect on distributions of precipitation, sea level, and many other phenomena are providing increasing reasons for caution and precautionary steps. The economic need to use alternative forms of energy also derives from the unavoidable loss, sooner or later, of the Earth's energy resources. Finally, the utilization of solar energy also constitutes a moral imperative when we consider our responsibilities to the generations to follow. Therefore, we have to research, develop, and test new solutions and new technologies. The possibilities presented by solar energy must be opened up by the energy sector, and we will need the best minds available to do this.

COMPARING SOLAR ENERGY AND FOSSIL FUELS

But why should all this be so difficult when the sun shines for free? The reason can be found in the low energy and power density of the incident solar radiation, as well as its irregularity. Imagine a cube of coal with sides measuring ten centimeters— this is much more than a kilogram of coal, which can produce roughly ten kilowatt hours of heat when burned. But you would be waiting a year for a two-dimensional surface with the same ten-centimeter sides to harvest the same amount of energy from the sun. When you fill up your automobile, 50 liters of gas flows into the tank in just a few minutes, and this is roughly equivalent to 600 kilowatt hours of energy. If you wanted to collect this amount of solar energy on the area of an automobile, roughly eight square meters, you would have to let it stand there for something like a month.

The advantage of fossil fuels is, therefore, their incredible energy density, created over geological time spans, even though it, too, ultimately comes from the sun. You can generalize this as follows: If nature assumes the job of collecting and concentrating solar energy, solar energy is favorably priced; if not, physics and technology have to come up with additional means, which have to be cheap enough, to make possible a more economical use of solar energy. . . .

HOUSING DESIGNS

The heating energy requirements of our houses represent the largest consumption sector in the energy field, as a result of which they play a very important role when it comes to carbon-dioxide emissions. But there is also a great deal of potential here for saving energy. If a house design takes into account the fact that the sun projects substantial amounts of energy onto the building's outer shell and exploits this solar advantage through careful planning and the use of the right technology, the heating energy requirement could be easily reduced by 50 percent or more compared with conventional building techniques. In Freiburg, Germany, the Fraunhofer Society has built a marvelous zero-energy house. The building has no connections with the electricity grid or energy supply network at all, but it does have remarkable heat insulation and a facade designed to make best use of the sun. This is not only true of the unusually rotund shape of the building's south side, but also of the transparent heat insulation covering the building's exterior. This material admits sunlight through the pipe structure made of polycarbonate or glass, but efficiently prevents heat loss to the outside, at night or on gloomy days, for example. The price of this material is continuing to fall.

The hot water supply at the house in Freiburg is generated by solar collectors on the roof and hot water boilers in the basement. The electricity supply is based on photovoltaic generators on the roof which do not only meet immediate needs but also charge up batteries for the night. They also operate an electrolysis unit to produce hydrogen which is stored for dark winter days. This very expensive step towards 100-percent self-sufficiency has been the subject of criticism because energy-independence geared to individual houses is not a rational model. Be that as it may, the house incorporates an entire range of technologies in an experimental, but highly intelligent, way. It also demonstrates that it is possible to design housing without an external, non-solar energy supply. Experimental houses of this kind—as well as their more economically viable relatives, i.e., low-energy houses which require a maximum of 7.5 liters of heating oil per square meter per year (a new norm for state subsidies)—do make great demands on construction physicists to the extent that they call for much more than relatively good heat insulation.

In the meantime, solar collectors are becoming a more common sight on rooftops. Not widely known is the fact that a small boom has also developed in Germany recently, with some 300,000 square meters of solar collectors being sold each year. Over one million square meters of collectors have now been installed, an area able to collect around one gigawatt of solar power, 30 to 40 percent of which can be delivered to the connected hot water systems. This is equal to roughly 300 million kilowatt hours of heat or 30 million liters of oil. In the future, there is significant potential not only in rooftop individual units, but also in large-scale solar collecting installations which would feed a district heating network for entire housing projects. There is also a need for some kind of seasonal hot water reservoir, of course, that would be able to store summer heat until winter comes around. This does not pose too great a problem, but it still has to be made considerably cheaper.

EFFICIENCY LEVELS

Photovoltaic technologies are no longer strange sights in public places. In many cities they can be found providing power for parking meters, and photovoltaic modules are sometimes also seen on roofs. Photovoltaic technology as such is still expensive, but it is especially viable in places which lack electricity cables, which are many, and is therefore opening up its first markets, in which photovoltaics is growing by roughly 15 percent a year and will soon be at a production figure of 100 megawatts a year. Europe is an important player in this field, with the Siemens-Solar company representing the world market leader.

Unfortunately, the theoretical efficiency levels of photovoltaics remain limited to roughly 30 percent. Of course such efficiency levels cannot be achieved in practical situations. Photovoltaic modules on the market today average roughly 12 to 16 percent. To improve effectiveness, then, an important developmental goal must be to develop another cheap materials and production process. A material in which great hopes are now being placed is copper-indium-diselenide. Even though the amount of energy needed in production should not be overlooked, it would appear that very high efficiency levels can be achieved on a reliable basis.

There is a particular problem here arising from the fact that the sun does not shine all the time, but we also need light and electricity at night. When solar or wind power is fed into the basic electricity network, you do not have to worry about it at first; at night, or when there is no wind, we can simply use electricity from the grid. I say "at first," because this will naturally only apply for as long as solar electricity plays a secondary role and coal-fired or nuclear power stations offer the security of supply. Economically, however, this means that solar electricity cannot be valued as highly as electricity from coal. In as much as we require not only power from our electricity grid, but also very exact frequencies and voltages, large quantities of solar or wind electricity involve new technological challenges which cannot be solved without additional financial outlay.

CLEAN AND CHEAP

Solar power technology is clean. Unlike coal, natural gas, or nuclear power, it emits no air pollutants or greenhouse gases, nor does it leave behind dangerous radioactive waste. And it doesn't require the construction of massive, expensive central power-generating stations or a nation-spanning electrical grid.

Now, with a speed catching many by surprise, our "solar future" may be upon us. Cheaper solar cell production processes; new, less expensive solar cell materials; the energy demands of the developing nations; and First World consumers' desire for clean energy could make solar power competitive with conventional technologies.

Randy Quinn, *World & I*, March 1997.

Where photovoltaic installations function without being connected to a power grid, expensive storage mechanisms can be avoided if the storage problem is moved to the production side of things. Water pumps or desalination plants powered by wind or photovoltaic technology provide good examples here: Water can simply be pumped into tanks in advance while the sun is shining or the wind blowing. As a result, photovoltaic water pumps are already a good market for photovoltaic technology in the developing world. Over the longer term, biomass—the solar energy stored in plants—will also play a greater role, so that combined biomass and solar installations could make other storage solutions superfluous; there is no other way of avoiding the necessity to employ batteries.

It is often claimed these days that such storage problems will not be solved without changing to a global hydrogen economy. Its supporters point out that hydrogen can be extracted from water, which is universally available, and that the end product of the environmentally friendly and carbon dioxide–free hydrogen combustion process is water. In other words, it is the ideal solution. Nevertheless, people should be warned against "hydrogen missionaries." There is a simple reason for this: You have to use nuclear power or renewable energy sources in order to produce hydrogen without generating any carbon dioxide, and, as a result, it must cost more than the primary energy used. From the solar energy perspective, this process demands increasing costs to produce a low-value fuel; everybody knows that they have to pay a lot more for a kilowatt hour of electricity than for a kilowatt hour of gas. Solar hydrogen will only be able to play a role in a world where the sun has finally become the dominant source of energy.

SOLAR POWER STATIONS

Solar-thermal electricity generation has now reached the power station market in California, where it is already generating roughly half of the world's solar electricity every year. These power stations focus the sun's rays through channels of mirrors, or troughs, onto a tube at their focal point, where a special oil is heated. The oil then releases its energy in a steam generator, which forms part of an almost conventional steam-power generating plant. But this process only works in direct sunlight in one of the world's sunbelts.

At the beginning of the 1990s, power stations of this type with a capacity of 354 megawatts were erected in California. These stations' essential components, especially the special mirrors, were produced in Germany, a country which also played a pioneering role in initial development in this field at the beginning of the 1980s.

At the solar test center near Almeria in southern Spain, various methods of solar-thermal electricity generation were compared in tests carried out with broad international participation under the auspices of the German Aerospace Research Agency (DLR). Today, the Plataforma Solar de Almeria (PSA) test center is still jointly operated by the DLR and the Spanish government, and it is also the place where Europe is advancing these promising technologies.

The history of these Californian power stations is both an encouraging success story and also a warning against failure in support policy. The state initially provided substantial subsidies to those who constructed the plants, but it gradually reduced this support. Through further development, the Luz company, a technologically and financially innovative operation, managed to reduce building costs so much that it was possible to build nine power stations with increasingly lower levels of state assistance. This continued until the last subsidies were cut back so sharply that further plants could no longer be completed and the Israeli-American company went under. The power stations are still in successful operation today. Despite the Luz company's economic failure, the success of these plants has motivated more than a few companies and research organizations to carry out further development. In Germany, this involves mainly the DLR, which is going forward with technical development, the Pilkington Group, and Siemens.

In a solar tower power plant also situated in California, a large number of mirrors arranged around the tower focus the sun's rays on the receiver at its top, where either liquid salt or air is heated—the former is the American answer to the problem, the latter the German. In both cases, heat exchangers transform the energy into steam for the generating process. The DLR and German industry have also made important contributions here. The economic prospects of this technology are similar to those of the "trough" power plants—time and the market will reveal the winner.

DIFFERENT TECHNOLOGIES FOR DIFFERENT INSTALLATIONS

Yet another somewhat similar technology is aimed at the market for decentralized units with a capacity of around ten kilowatts. Three German-built installations with parabolic mirrors and a Stirling engine at their respective focal points are also being tested at the PSA by DLR. Systems of this sort, generally referred to as dish-stirling installations, are no more economical than photovoltaic systems when produced in individual units, as has been the case so far, but major savings are foreseen through mass production and a number of innovations currently being developed. Finally, let me mention a German development which has often attracted attention because of its spectacular dimensions, but also engenders some skepticism, namely, [an] updraft power station. This is based on an idea which has been confirmed in theory and by experiment: A tower of up to 1,000 meters high works like a chimney while the sun heats the air around it under a greenhouse-like glass and foil roof. The hot air surges up and turns turbines inside the tower, which in turn convert this energy into electricity for the grid.

This last technology uses very simply designed collectors and can also be made very cheaply, especially in the developing world. There again, its solar-electric efficiency is rather low, at roughly one percent. At the other end of the scale is dish-stirling technology. Its more complex optical elements make the collection of solar energy expensive, but also make it possible to attain the highest efficiency ratings of all solar-electric technologies, at more than 30 percent. Solar tower and paraboloid troughs take up the middle ground with regard to their collector complexity and efficiency. Photovoltaics will only be able to compete with large-scale electricity generation when producing appropriate solar cells is as cheap as the parabolic mirrors used in solar-thermal power stations. For small installations under five kilowatts, photovoltaic technology is the clear winner among solar technologies, whereas dish systems have favorable prospects when capacities of between 10 and 30 kilowatts are called for.

In as much as all of these technologies are required for the sustainable, environmentally harmonious development of humankind—for the second solar civilization—they still have to be made considerably cheaper, something which won't be possible without the commitment of the best physicists and engineers. It has been said that the 20th century is the century of the electron—the 21st will be the century of the photon, including solar photons, from which humankind must once again learn to live.

"Wind power . . . could become an important energy source for many nations within the next decade."

THE USE OF WIND POWER SHOULD BE INCREASED

Christopher Flavin

Many nations are harnessing wind power for their energy needs. In the following viewpoint, Christopher Flavin argues that wind energy could soon become an important energy source throughout the world. Flavin contends that technological improvements stand to make wind power one of the world's most economical sources for electricity. Although the growth of the wind power industry has slowed in the United States, he maintains, it has emerged and promises to grow in many developing nations. Flavin is a researcher for the Worldwatch Institute, a Washington, D.C., organization that conducts research on global and ecological problems.

As you read, consider the following questions:

1. According to Flavin, how many wind turbines are now in operation?
2. What will drive the demand for wind power in developing nations, according to Flavin?
3. What percentage of the world's electricity could be produced by wind power, in the author's opinion?

W ind power is now the world's fastest growing energy source. Global wind power generating capacity rose to 4,900 megawatts at the end of 1995, up from 3,700 megawatts a year earlier. Since 1990, total installed wind power capacity has risen by 150 percent, representing an annual growth rate of 20 percent.

By contrast, nuclear power is growing at a rate of less than 1 percent per year, while world coal combustion has not grown at all in the 1990s.

If the world's roughly 25,000 wind turbines were spinning simultaneously, they could light 122 million 40-watt light bulbs or power over a million suburban homes. In the windy north German state of Schleswig-Holstein, wind power already provides 8 percent of the electricity.

Although it now generates less than 1 percent of the world's electricity, the rapid growth and steady technological advance of wind power suggest that it could become an important energy source for many nations within the next decade. The computer industry has demonstrated the potentially powerful impact of double digit growth rates. The fact that personal computers provided less than 1 percent of world computing power in 1980 did not prevent them—a decade later—from dominating the industry, and changing the very nature of work.

Wind power is being propelled largely by its environmental advantages. Unlike coal-fired power plants, the leading source of electricity today, wind power produces no health-damaging air pollution or acid rain. Nor does it produce carbon dioxide—the leading greenhouse gas now destabilizing the world's atmosphere.

In many regions, wind power is now competitive with new fossil fuel–fired power plants. At an average wind speed of 6 meters per second (13 miles per hour) wind power now costs 5–7 cents per kilowatt-hour, similar or slightly lower than the range for new coal plants. As wind turbines are further improved, with lighter and more aerodynamic blades as well as better control systems, and as they are produced in greater quantity, costs could fall even further, making wind power one of the world's most economical electricity sources.

WIND POWER'S ROOTS

The modern wind power industry established its roots in Denmark and California in the early 1980s. Spurred by government research funds, generous tax incentives, and guaranteed access to the electricity grids, a sizable wind industry was created. However, development slowed dramatically at the end of the decade as government tax incentives were withdrawn and utilities became more resistant to higher-cost electricity.

Even as political support for wind power waned in the late 1980s, the technology continued to mature. Many of the small turbines installed in the early days were expensive and unreliable, but the lessons learned from those first generation turbines were soon translated into new and improved models. The turbines that entered the market in the early 1990s incorporated advanced synthetic materials, sophisticated electronic controls, and the latest in aerodynamic designs.

WIND GENERATING CAPACITY BY REGION, 1980–95

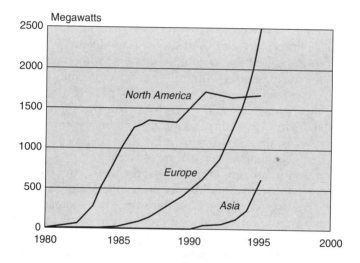

Source: Madsen, Gipe and Associates.

In an effort to make wind power more economical, most companies have built larger and larger turbines. In Germany, the average turbine installed in 1995 had a capacity of 480 kilowatts, up from 370 kilowatts in 1994 and 180 kilowatts in 1992. Several manufacturers will soon introduce machines that can generate between 1,000 and 1,500 kilowatts—with blade spans as great as 65 meters.

The 1,290 megawatts of wind generating capacity added in 1995 was almost double the capacity added a year earlier, and up sixfold from the 1990 figure. In 1995, the country with the most new capacity was again Germany, which added 505 megawatts, the most any country has ever installed in a single year.

India added 375 megawatts, followed by Denmark with 98 new megawatts, Netherlands with 95, and Spain with 58.

EUROPE'S LEADERSHIP

The European wind industry is now growing at an explosive pace: altogether, Europe had 2,500 megawatts of wind power capacity at the end of 1995, up nearly threefold from 860 megawatts in 1992. The United States still led the world with 1,650 megawatts of wind power capacity at the end of 1995, but Germany was closing in fast with 1,130 megawatts. Denmark ranked third with 610 megawatts, and India fourth at 580 megawatts.

Europe is now home to most of the world's leading wind power companies, which are introducing larger and more cost-effective models. Unlike the United States, where most development has consisted of large groups of 20 to 100 turbines, called "wind farms," Denmark and Germany have pursued a decentralized approach to wind power development. Most of their machines are installed one or two at a time, across the rural landscape. This has made them popular with local communities, which benefit from the additional income, public revenues, and jobs that result.

Europe's leadership also stems from the financial incentives and high purchase prices established for renewable energy in response to concern about the atmospheric pollution caused by fossil fuel–fired power plants. In Germany, this approach has allowed determined investors and environmental advocates to beat back efforts by the electric utilities to reverse the 1991 "electricity in-feed law," which provides a generous price of about 11 cents per kilowatt-hour to electricity generators relying on solar, wind, and biomass energy. In a landmark vote in 1995, the Bundestag [the lower house of Germany's parliament] decided to uphold the law, though it remains under review by the courts.

Wind energy is also advancing rapidly in the Netherlands, Spain, and the United Kingdom. The U.K. has Europe's largest wind power potential, and hundreds of megawatts of projects are now being planned. European wind industry leaders are also hopeful that sizable wind power markets will soon emerge in Finland, Greece, Ireland, and Sweden, each of which has a large wind resource. Even France, the last bastion of the European nuclear industry, embarked on a sizable wind power development plan in 1995, aimed at adding 250 to 450 megawatts of wind power over the next decade.

Just as wind energy development is taking off in Europe, it

has stalled in the United States, where the industry is buffeted by uncertainty about the future structure of the electricity industry. In fact, the country's total wind capacity has hardly increased since 1991. The country that led the world into wind power in the 1980s actually saw a net decline of 8 megawatts in its installed capacity in 1995. Some 50 megawatts were added—mainly in Texas—but 58 megawatts of old turbines were torn down in California. Kenetech, the leading U.S. wind power company, filed for bankruptcy in May 1996 after the combined effects of a slow market and mechanical problems with its new turbine led to large financial losses.

GREAT POTENTIAL

Excluding environmentally sensitive areas, the global wind energy potential is roughly five times current global electricity use. Since the power available from wind rises with the cube of the wind speed, most of the development will occur in particularly windy areas. In the United States, where detailed surveys have been conducted, it appears that wind turbines installed on 0.6 percent of the land area of the 48 contiguous states—mainly in the Great Plains—could meet 20 percent of current U.S. power needs.

Christopher Flavin and Nicholas Lenssen, *Power Surge*, 1994.

Prospects for developing nations are far brighter. Although most wind turbines are currently installed in industrial countries, much of the world's wind power potential is in the developing world. The leader so far is India, which is the first developing country with a real commercial market for wind power. India's roughly 3,000 wind turbines have virtually all been installed since the government opened the electricity grid to independent power producers and enacted tax incentives for renewable energy investments in the early 1990s. According to the government, 730 megawatts had been installed by April 1, 1996, which would make India the world's most active wind market in early 1996. However, uncertainty surrounding the Indian elections in May 1996 has slowed the pace of development since then.

Some of India's wind turbines are being imported, but others are manufactured in India, either by domestic companies or in joint ventures with foreign companies. Already, the Indian industry has more than 20 indigenous manufacturers and suppliers. In the windy southern state of Tamil Nadu, hundreds of jobs have been created as a result.

Many other developing countries, including Argentina, Brazil, China, Egypt, Mexico, and the Philippines are surveying their wind resources and installing small numbers of turbines on an experimental basis. Although none of these countries has yet encouraged or even permitted the development of a sustained, market-driven wind industry, some may be on the verge. China, for example, has just 36 megawatts installed but has plans to reach 1,000 megawatts by the year 2000.

In most developing countries, wind power development will be driven not by environmental concerns, as it is in industrial countries, but by a desperate need for electricity, which is in short supply throughout the Third World. In areas such as western China and northeast Brazil, wind power is the only indigenous source of electricity ready to be developed on a large scale.

WIND ENERGY POTENTIAL

The global wind energy potential is roughly five times current global electricity use—even excluding environmentally sensitive areas. In the United States, where detailed surveys have been conducted, it appears that wind turbines installed on 0.6 percent of the land area of the 48 contiguous states—mainly in the Great Plains—could meet one-fifth of current U.S. power needs—double the current contribution of hydropower. By comparison, the total cropland used to grow corn in the United States is nearly 3 percent of the country's land area. And unlike corn, wind power does not preclude the land from being used simultaneously for other purposes, including agriculture and grazing.

Other countries that have enough wind potential to supply most or all their electricity include Argentina, Canada, Chile, Russia, and the United Kingdom. China's wind energy potential is estimated by the government at 253,000 megawatts, which exceeds the country's current generating capacity from all sources by 40 percent. Much of that potential is located in Inner Mongolia, near some of the country's leading industrial centers.

India's potential is estimated at 80,000 megawatts, which equals the country's total current generating capacity. Europe could obtain between 7 and 26 percent of its power from the wind, depending on how much land is excluded for environmental reasons. Offshore potential in Europe's North and Baltic Seas is even greater.

Wind power cannot fully replace fossil fuels, but it has the potential to meet or exceed the 20 percent of world electricity provided by hydropower. Moreover, though wind power is more abundant in some areas than others, it is in fact one of the world's most widely distributed energy resources. More countries have wind power potential than have large resources of hydropower or coal.

Combined with other renewable energy sources such as solar and geothermal power, and by a new generation of gas-fired micro-power plants located in office and apartment buildings, wind power could help transform the world electricity system. These technologies could quickly replace coal and nuclear power—which together now supply two-thirds of the world's electricity—and allow a sharp reduction in world carbon emissions.

| "The welfare of our future generations and the environment may depend on maintaining the viability of nuclear power."

THE USE OF NUCLEAR POWER SHOULD BE INCREASED

Bertram Wolfe

Bertram Wolfe, a former president of the American Nuclear Society and a former general manager of General Electric's nuclear energy division, is a consultant in Monte Sereno, California. In the following viewpoint, Wolfe argues that future population growth will lead to sharply increasing demands for energy. Wolfe contends that because of the environmental problems associated with fossil fuels, the United States should meet this growing energy demand with nuclear energy, which he says is a proven and reliable energy source. Wolfe asserts that nuclear energy plants meeting U.S. standards have an untarnished safety record and that the storage of nuclear waste is a manageable problem. Wolfe contends that issues of safety and storage should not prevent government from increasing the supply of nuclear energy.

As you read, consider the following questions:

1. What is the difference between the amount of energy produced by breeder reactors and conventional reactors, according to Wolfe?
2. According to Wolfe, what does the Advanced Liquid Metal Reactor (ALMR) do to radioactive materials?
3. In the author's opinion, what increases the threat that nuclear weapons will be acquired and used?

Third World population growth and economic development are setting the stage for an energy crisis in the 21st century. By mid-century the Third World population will double from 4 billion to 8 billion people, while the population of the industrial world will grow by about 20 percent to 1.2 billion. Impoverished Third World people today use less than one-tenth as much energy per capita as do U.S. citizens. Unless we expect to see the majority of the world's people living indefinitely in dire poverty, we should be prepared for per capita energy use to rise rapidly with economic progress. Even if Third World per capita energy use rises to only one-third of the U.S. level, that increase in combination with expected population growth will result in a threefold increase in world energy use by 2050.

If fossil fuels are used to supply this increased energy need, we can expect serious deterioration of air quality and possible environmental disaster from global climate change due to the greenhouse effect. In addition, increased demand for fossil fuels combined with dwindling supplies will lead to higher prices, slowed economic growth, and the likelihood of energy-related global conflicts. Does anyone doubt that Kuwait's oil resources were a major factor in U.S. willingness to take military action against Iraq? Increased competition for fossil fuels will only exacerbate tensions.

Alternatives to this scenario are few. Perhaps future world energy use can be stabilized at a level much less than a third of present U.S. per capita use. (Of course, the demand could be much higher.) Perhaps solar or wind power will become practical on a large scale. Perhaps fusion, or even cold fusion, will be developed. Perhaps some new, clean, plentiful energy source will emerge. We can all hope for an easy answer to our energy needs, but it is irresponsible to base our future on such hopes.

FOCUS ON NUCLEAR POWER

But if we limit our planning to proven and reliable energy technologies with adequate fuel supplies and low environmental risks that we know can meet the world's energy needs in the 21st century, we must focus on nuclear power. However, even conventional nuclear power plants will face fuel supply problems in the 21st century if their use expands significantly. Fortunately, we also have experience with nuclear breeder reactors, such as the Advanced Liquid Metal Reactor (ALMR), that can produce more than a hundred times as much energy per pound of uranium as do conventional reactors.

The United States has been a leader in the development of

nuclear power technology and the adoption of stringent safety standards. Not a single member of the public has been harmed by the operation of any of the world's nuclear plants that meet U.S. standards. (The Chernobyl reactor, which lacked a containment structure, did not meet U.S. standards.) The United States has also been successful in using its peaceful nuclear power leadership to limit the worldwide spread of nuclear weapons.

But the future of nuclear energy in the United States is now in question. Since 1973, all new nuclear energy plant orders have subsequently been canceled. In 1993, U.S. utilities shut down three nuclear energy plants rather than invest in needed repairs. Of the 110 presently operating U.S. nuclear energy plants, 45 will reach the end of their planned 40-year lifetime in the next two decades, and there are no plans for replacing them with new nuclear energy plants. Indeed, the utility industry seems to have no interest in even thinking about building new nuclear power plants. Not a single U.S. utility responded to a Nuclear Regulatory Commission (NRC) request to test a proposed new procedure for early approval of a new nuclear energy plant site even though no commitment for actual site use was required. And the Bill Clinton administration has canceled support for advanced nuclear energy development programs, including the ALMR program.

THE ATTRACTIVENESS OF NUCLEAR POWER

This is the wrong time for the nation or the world to ignore nuclear power. Demand for energy will grow, and our options are limited. Ironically, environmentalists, who have opposed nuclear power since the 1970s, should have the strongest rationale for promoting nuclear energy. Like almost all large endeavors, nuclear power has its problems and its risks. But the problems of nuclear power do not look so bad when compared with the air pollution, global warming, and the supply limitations associated with fossil fuels. Besides, the major drawbacks of nuclear power—from cost to waste disposal—are due more to institutional impediments than to technological difficulties. Considering the growth in energy demand and the risks associated with other energy sources, the benefit-risk ratio for nuclear power is very attractive. Indeed, the welfare of our future generations and the environment may depend on maintaining the viability of nuclear power. . . .

U.S. nuclear power plants themselves have an admirable environmental and public health record. Safety has been a critical consideration in plant design from the beginning. Standard operation of a nuclear plant produces no ill effects, and even in the case of a major malfunction or accident, the use of a containment structure that surrounds the plant prevents the release of significant amounts of radioactive material. The wisdom of the U.S. approach is evident in a comparison of the accidents at the Three Mile Island plant in Pennsylvania [in 1979] and the Soviet Union's Chernobyl reactor [in 1986]. Thanks to the containment structure, not a single member of the public was injured by nuclear radiation from the Three Mile Island accident. In fact, a person standing outside the plant would have received less radiation exposure from it than from a two-week vacation in high-altitude Denver with its uranium-rich soil. Significant harm to humans resulted from the accident at the Chernobyl plant, which lacked a containment structure.

MANAGING NUCLEAR WASTE

One commonly cited drawback of nuclear power is that it creates radioactive waste that must be contained for thousands of years. Nuclear waste is a serious concern, but one that can be successfully managed and is less worrisome than the emissions from fossil-fuel plants. Coal, gas, wood, and oil plants emit greenhouse gases and other undesirable materials to the environment. No nuclear wastes are directly emitted to the environment. Of course, radioactive waste can represent a serious hazard if it is not properly maintained, but its small volume allows very high expenditures and great care per unit volume. If all the country's high-level nuclear waste from over three decades of plant operations were collected on a football field, it would be only 9 feet deep. Nuclear power plant wastes have been carefully maintained at the plants for decades without harm to the environment or the public. Because high-level waste, composed largely of spent nuclear fuel, remains radioactive for thousands of years, the plan is to seal this waste in sturdy containers and bury it in underground geological structures that have remained stable for millions of years. The feasibility of this approach has been supported by a large number of national and international studies.

After the Department of Energy considered a number of possible storage sites for the waste and made its recommendations, Congress selected Yucca Mountain, Nevada, which is adjacent to a nuclear weapons testing site, as the place for the first high-level waste repository. Extensive underground exploration of the site and evaluation of its geology is now under way. If this research finds that the site is suitable, the repository will begin operation in the period from 2010 to 2020. In the meantime, the used fuel can be safely stored indefinitely in above-ground facilities.

Progress toward permanent storage of low-level waste from nuclear energy plants, medical procedures, and industrial processes, which is less radioactive and loses its radioactivity within a few hundred years, has also been slow. In 1987, Congress passed a law giving responsibility for management of the low-level wastes to the states. What has happened since then in California is an example of the institutional barriers impeding nuclear power development.

RIGHT DIRECTION, SLOW PACE

After extensive study, California chose a site in Ward Valley in the Mojave desert. The California Department of Health Services spent several years reviewing the site and the design of the repository, with ample opportunities for public input. In 1993, it approved the site and design. Unfortunately, the site is on federal land, which must be transferred to the state before it can be used for the repository. Secretary of the Interior Bruce Babbitt insisted on an independent review by the National Research Council before making the transfer. This year-long study concluded in May 1995 that the site was suitable for the repository. Similar conclusions were also reached by the Bureau of Land Management and the U.S. Geological Survey. Nevertheless, because of pressure from antinuclear organizations, the site has still not been transferred, and it is not clear how long the delay will be. In the meantime, the low-level wastes, including medical and industrial wastes, are being held at many temporary storage sites in the state. These sites could raise safety problems that would easily be avoided by opening the Ward Valley Repository.

A BRIGHT FUTURE

In a more rational world to come, nuclear energy should have a bright future. Reactors, factory-built to a standard design, will reduce cost and increase safety. Uranium is plentiful and cheap, and likely to be so for many decades. The dismantling of nuclear weapons is releasing high quality fissionable materials for peaceful reactors, industry is learning to extend reactor life and the burn-up time of fuels—again lowering costs.

S. Fred Singer, *Washington Times*, August 18, 1995.

There is no guarantee of absolute safety with nuclear wastes or with any potentially hazardous substance. Numerous expert studies have found that Yucca Mountain and Ward Valley provide the safety needed by the public. But as long as our institutional processes make it easy to stop the development of repositories on the basis of insubstantial doubts about safety, we will not be able to move from temporary storage to a safer, permanent solution. We are moving in the right direction, but the pace is unnecessarily slow. And while antinuclear activists continue to quibble about the possibility of some future hazard, we continue to pollute the air with fossil fuel emissions that cause tens of thousands of premature deaths each year in the United States and produce greenhouse gases that could lead to global climate change with potentially disastrous consequences. Are some environmental Neros fiddling while Rome burns?

And if high-level radioactive waste is such a serious problem, doesn't it make sense to revive developmental support for the ALMR reactor, which "burns" or transmutes the long-lived radioactive materials, so that after a few hundred years the wastes become less hazardous than the natural uranium in the ground?

REVIVING NUCLEAR POWER

As the damaging effects of fossil fuels become more apparent and the need for additional electric generating capacity increases, the time for dismissing nuclear power is coming to an end. The current generation of U.S. nuclear power plants has performed well, and an even better generation of new designs is ready. General Electric, in partnership with Hitachi and Toshiba, has developed the Advanced Boiling Water Reactor (ABWR), which incorporates lessons learned from earlier designs. Construction of the first ABWR began in Japan in 1991, and the plant is already operating at full power. The ability to build and begin operation of a new design in less than five years is a testament to the quality of construction and the regulatory system in Japan. Combustion Engineering, which has been building its System 80 nuclear plants in South Korea in less than six years, is ready to move forward with its improved System 80+. Both of these new designs have already gone through more than six years of evaluation by NRC, receiving favorable reviews and approvals.

In addition to these evolutionary new designs, several companies have been working on passively safe designs, which it is hoped will provide even greater protection in the event of an accident. Westinghouse's AP600 and the technology of General Electric's Simplified Boiling Water Reactor (SBWR) are moving forward, but neither design is ready for commercial construction. Although there are people who argue that we should wait for such designs to be ready before building any new nuclear plants in the United States, currently available designs do not pose a safety problem and are safer than the alternative of increased fossil fuel use. Thus, there is no practical reason to wait for a new design that is theoretically safer but has its own development problems.

Reviews of the new commercially available designs indicate that they will have favorable safety, operating, and economic characteristics compared to fossil plants if (and this is a big if) they can be built as efficiently here as they are in other countries. But experience with the U.S. licensing and court review procedures suggests that it can take two to four times as long to construct a nuclear plant in the United States as it does abroad, with exorbitant increases in cost. . . .

Japan, Korea, and France have demonstrated that nuclear power plants that meet U.S. standards can be built economically in four to six years. Thus our problem is clearly not technical but institutional: Can we build U.S.-designed plants as efficiently in the United States as we do abroad? Our government should eliminate bureaucratic impediments that serve only as tools for those philosophically opposed to nuclear power.

LONG-TERM NEEDS

The world must be prepared for the increasing energy needs in the 21st century and beyond. The U.S.-led ALMR program was intended to develop a safe, economical, proliferation-resistant, essentially unlimited energy supply for the future. The program was proceeding well, with reactor design and fuel cycle development making substantial progress. As we have learned from past experience with light water reactors, it takes decades to uncover and solve the long-term problems of a new nuclear system. Thus, to be ready for the energy needs projected in the 21st century, the ALMR development program should be vigorously pursued now. Private companies cannot take on such an expensive and slow-maturing project. Government must fund the project at this stage.

Unfortunately, the program has been canceled because of concern that the use of plutonium could lead to the proliferation of nuclear weapons. Although it is true that the use of breeder reactors in the United States would result in the creation of more plutonium, a U.S. decision to forgo breeder reactors will not affect other countries that see the need for breeders in the future and continue to develop and operate them. The major effect of our abandonment of the ALMR program will be loss of U.S. leadership and influence in its future development as well as the loss of our leadership in assuring a proliferation-resistant fuel cycle. Besides, the failure to provide adequate and affordable electricity for future economic needs is a much more serious threat to world peace. Indeed, competition and potential hostilities over scarce energy supplies increase the threat that nuclear weapons will be acquired—and used.

None of these policy changes will be made without a change in the public's attitude toward nuclear power. People need to understand the need for additional future energy supplies; the problems of fossil fuels; and the relative safety, reliability, and environmental advantages of nuclear power. The nuclear industry has done a poor job of educating the public about nuclear energy. And because of its perceived economic stake, the nuclear industry may not be a credible carrier for this message. More disinterested voices, particularly those in the environmental community, should be heard. The Club of Rome, an international organization with a particular interest in preserving the environment, has evolved from nuclear critic to nuclear promoter because of its concern about global climate change. U.S. environmentalists need to take a fresh look at world and national energy needs, the clear and worsening problems of fossil fuels, and the empirical evidence about the safety of nuclear power.

"It's at least 95 percent less polluting
to drive an electric car versus an
internal-combustion engine."

ELECTRIC VEHICLES ARE AN EFFICIENT ALTERNATIVE TO GAS CARS

Ed Begley Jr., interviewed by Dick Russell

Ed Begley Jr. is a television and motion picture actor who starred in the television series *St. Elsewhere*. Dick Russell is a freelance writer in Boston. In the following viewpoint, excerpted from an interview in *E Magazine*, Begley describes his commitment to drive electric vehicles, which he asserts do not pollute the air as do fossil-fuel-powered vehicles. Begley maintains that although the major American auto manufacturers are uninterested in promoting electric cars, other companies are building these vehicles and improving electric batteries to increase their mileage range.

As you read, consider the following questions:

1. What does Begley say caused him to become concerned about the environment?
2. How does Begley recharge his electric vehicle?
3. In Begley's opinion, why have America's automakers been reluctant to develop electric vehicles?

From Ed Begley Jr., interview by Dick Russell, "Conversations: Ed Begley Jr.," E/The Environmental Magazine, February 1996. Reprinted with permission from: E/The Environmental Magazine, Subscription Dept., PO Box 2047, Marion, OH 43306. (815) 734-1242.

In Hollywood, where environmentalism is chic but lip-service is the pervading reality, Ed Begley, Jr. is one actor whose uncompromising personal commitment goes without saying. To say that Begley practices what he preaches is putting it mildly. His ranch-style solar-energized home in the San Fernando Valley is entirely off the power grid. With rare exceptions, Begley refuses even to ride in a gasoline-powered automobile. He drives an electric car to film shoots. On the road, he takes public transportation or peddles around a fold-up bicycle that can be assembled in 20 seconds. Begley's weekly generation of garbage fits snugly into the small glove compartment of his electric car; he recycles or composts nearly all of his household waste.

Best known for his starring role on the TV series *St. Elsewhere*, Begley is also one of five appointed Environmental Commissioners for the city of Los Angeles and currently sits on the boards of five environmental organizations—The American Oceans Campaign, Santa Monica Mountains Conservancy, League of Conservation Voters, Environmental Research Foundation and the Walden Woods Project. . . .

BEGLEY'S ENVIRONMENTAL MINDSET

Russell: How was it that you became such a wonderful fanatic about the environment? Was it something that happened in your early years, or something you read?

Begley: It was a series of events, but a big part of it was scouting in my youth. This was back in the late 50s when my family lived on Long Island. Anyone camping in those wild and beautiful areas couldn't help but grow up with a profound respect for natural systems. I doubt if [conservative commentators] John Sununu or Rush Limbaugh were ever in the Boy Scouts.

When I was about 13, we moved back to California where I was born and I saw the way the San Fernando Valley had already begun to change from a basically rural area to all these shopping malls. Plus, when I ran down to my friend's house, I found I could barely breathe. The smog was choking us in the early 60s. Then I'd go out to Santa Monica Bay and witness this incredible pollution.

In 1969 came those Hasselblad pictures taken during the first moonwalk, of this beautiful frail water planet in the distance. This had a profound impact on many people I knew—seeing the Earth as a whole, and us as a part of a finite region. By the time the first Earth Day happened in 1970, I was poised to really get involved. That's when I became a vegetarian, started recycling and composting, and bought my first electric car.

You bought an electric car 25 years ago?

Yep, it was a Taylor-Dunn, made by a company that's still in business. They basically built glorified golf carts for hauling stuff around industrial complexes. It cost me $900 or so. It was pretty slow and didn't go very far, but it met my needs. I stopped driving it after awhile, when somebody told me I wasn't really doing anything about air pollution because the power plant created just as much as an auto tailpipe. That wasn't true, but I didn't know anything about electric power generation at the time, or the plans put into effect a few years later to change over a lot of the coal-burning plants to natural gas and hydroelectric. The fact is, every study that's been done shows it's at least 95 percent less polluting to drive an electric car versus an internal-combustion engine. Do you realize that you use 25 percent of your gasoline in a big city *stopped* in traffic? Now I'm on my third electric vehicle, a converted VW Rabbit that runs like a top.

MANY POWER SOURCES

Unlike conventional vehicles, which run almost exclusively on petroleum-based fuels, electric vehicles [EVs] are able to tap into a large number of power sources, including renewables such as hydro, wind, geothermal, and biomass. In a demonstration project run by the Massachusetts energy office, solar cells provide the electricity to recharge EVs parked at two commuter rail train stations in the Boston area. Solar panels on the roofs of houses could collect solar energy by day and use it to charge a spare EV battery. Once home, the motorist would simply exchange today's spent battery pack with the newly charged one.

Drew Kodjak, *Technology Review*, August/September 1996.

Do you have a recharging area at home? And what about the inconvenience of getting around L.A. to film shoots?

At night I just plug into a regular 110-volt outlet in my garage. And electric vehicle charging stations are popping up like mushrooms all over L.A. now, in key locations. You plug in for free, courtesy of the Department of Water and Power. Ninety percent of our trips are 40 miles or less. Well, even the most lame-ass electric car can go that far without a recharge.

The incentive plan in L.A. is to have electric vehicle parking spaces similar to those for handicapped parking, and to allow you to drive in the diamond lane on the freeways. All this is going to add up to people wanting these cars. If General Motors [GM] won't do it, then Peugeot has one for $10,000. [Editor's note: Electric versions of the Peugeot 106 and Citroen AX with nickel-cadmium batteries are already on sale in Europe, though there are no current plans to sell them in the U.S. CALSTART's CITI two-passenger electric car will, however, be sold on the U.S. market for less than $10,000.]

Who Will Take the Lead?

Why did the Big Three automakers resist—and help kill—the mandates in California and several Northeastern states that would require about 70,000 electric vehicles to be manufactured by 1998 and nearly a million by 2003?

They're resistant to change. They fought against seat belts and airbags, and they're fighting electric cars now. I've been told that a lot of the same individuals are on the boards of both the big oil companies and the automakers, which of course is one factor. But I can see why they're scared. California, Massachusetts and New York comprise 38 percent of the domestic market for automobiles. Even though the mandates call for only two percent of that 38 percent to be electric, that's still a big number.

I think the automakers are afraid of the same situation they ran into in the early 60s, when there was so much pressure to build a fuel-efficient car like the Volkswagen. The best they could come up with was the Corvair, which wasn't a very good car. So they said, see, it can't be done. Well, companies in Japan, Germany and other countries stepped in and gave us safe, fuel-efficient cars that ran very well. We've been playing catch-up ever since.

It's hard to know who will take the lead. Look what happened in the computer industry. Who was Compaq or Bill Gates 12 years ago? The big players a while back were RCA and Atari. IBM farmed out this whole "nuisance area" called software to Bill Gates, figuring they made the box and so were the ones in charge. That's been quite an upheaval. But certain departments at General Motors are actually gung-ho. Bob Stempel, who formerly ran GM, is now head of a partnership that makes a new nickel–metal hydride battery.

Isn't battery technology still the biggest obstacle to moving forward more rapidly, given the limited range of what's available today?

Yes, but that's changing. Stempel's Ovonics battery has tested out at a 200-mile range in one competition. There's another company, Electro-Source, that makes a sealed lead-acid battery that's easy to charge and is being made in quantity. If you put those batteries in the Impact electric car that GM is working on, I would guess you're going to get a 130- or 140-mile range.

Transportation Concerns

But despite the advantages in terms of pollution, aren't electric vehicles really secondary to improvements in public transportation?

I agree. Electric vehicles do nothing to alleviate traffic congestion. I mean, the automobile was our dearest lover and now it's a fatal attraction of the worst order. In California, where the automobile was first promoted as the center of American life, that dream was also based on subterfuge and deceit. Back in the 1940s, this cabal of GM, Standard Oil of New Jersey, Firestone Tires and Mack Trucks bought up the public transportation systems not only in L.A. but a number of states. Now we're fighting tooth and nail in L.A. to try to build a 1990s version of the old red-car trolleys that they tore down. Nobody wants it aboveground anywhere near them, because there's no history that people remember. So you've got to dig a hole in the ground, which is a lot more expensive, and put the system down there. That's what we're faced with, because of what was foisted upon us almost 50 years ago.

Amazing, you may be the only person in America who takes his personal ethic that far. Getting back to the politics of all this, what do you think of the Bill Clinton administration's Partnership for a New Generation of Vehicles, with this 80-mile-per-gallon goal that is being called for?

I'm encouraged by that, though I don't want it to distract from the electric vehicle programs. Isn't it interesting that the auto companies claimed for years that they couldn't beat the laws of physics to make such a highly fuel-efficient car? Now they're saying, well, just get away from these damned electric cars and we'll give you an internal-combustion engine that gets 70 miles to the gallon. So why not do both?

> "[Bicycles are] the most efficient and effective form of personal transportation ever conceived."

BICYCLES ARE AN EFFICIENT ALTERNATIVE TO AUTOMOBILES

Rémi Tremblay

Bicycles, or "human-powered vehicles" (HPVs), could become an alternative to the ever-growing number of automobiles worldwide, Rémi Tremblay argues in the following viewpoint. Tremblay contends that the increased use of bicycles instead of cars as a mode of transportation would drastically reduce society's dependence on crude oil and would ease air pollution and other environmental problems. Tremblay is an editor of the quarterly magazine *Creation Spirituality Network*.

As you read, consider the following questions:

1. How much of America's urban space is used to accommodate automobiles, according to Tremblay?
2. According to Tremblay, how can HPVs revitalize cities?
3. In the author's opinion, what infrastructure is needed to encourage HPV commuting?

From Rémi Tremblay, "Reinventing the Wheel: Returning to a More Spirit-Filled Mode of Transportation," *Creation Spirituality Network*, Fall 1996. Reprinted by permission of the author.

Each day in the US, 135 million cars clog the highways and roads consuming about 8 million barrels of fuel. The average American spends up to 20 percent of annual household expenses on auto-related expenses and puts in 400 hours each year in driving time with the estimated average speed of 5 mph (after figuring in driving time plus time spent dealing with cars). Globally, 90 percent of the carbon monoxide produced is attributable to transportation. Six of the seven chief air pollutants come from automobiles. Running on a summer day in an urban area for only 30 minutes is equivalent to smoking a pack of cigarettes. Motor vehicle damage to human health and the environment is estimated at up to $93 billion per year in the US. Excluding the 11 million gallons of oil leaked from the Exxon Valdez in March 1989, 766 vessel accidents in the first half of 1989 resulted in 5.8 million gallons of oil being spilled into US waters. Of the 6 million underground oil and gasoline storage tanks in the US, it is thought that 500,000 are leaking. More people have been killed in automobile accidents than in all the wars fought by this county in the past 200 years (43,134 traffic fatalities in 1994, up from 42,750 in 1993). Close to half of all urban space in the US goes to accommodate the automobile which leaves more land devoted to cars than to housing. Pavement now covers 10 percent of all the arable land in the US. Our country spends nearly $200 million per day building and rebuilding roads. Nearly 100,000 people a year are displaced in the US by new highway construction.

THE ILLUSION SURROUNDING CARS

Faced with such statistics, North Americans would do well to question our infatuation with cars. They are killing us faster than all the wars we've fought. They are extremely expensive to own and operate. They are destroying our cities and the environment. And they are excruciating to drive in urban areas. What can possibly attract us to these machines? The simple answer is that we live in a culture carefully crafted around the illusion that cars are necessary. An unprecedented amount of time, energy, and money is spent each year to convince us that cars are a natural extension of our individual minds, bodies, and souls. We are told that if we do not own a car, we will never be able to reach the ecstatic joy of becoming an achieved human being, free from all bondage; and, of course, the more powerful and luxurious the car is, the more we will surpass our mundane existence. Cars are not merely tools to facilitate transportation, but soulmates that magically enhance our sense of being, freedom, and pleasure.

Another factor in our continuing love affair with cars is that we are kept in the dark about the real costs of owning and operating such a vehicle. When buying or using a car, we are not warned of its ill effects on our health and the environment. The EPA reports that 55 percent of the cancer attributed to air pollution is the result of emissions from road vehicles including both passenger cars and diesel trucks. Prior to 1993, car manufacturers in Detroit spent $20 million trying to prevent the introduction of air bags. Public health is not a high priority in the carmakers' agenda. Nor does the price of gasoline reflect the real cost of driving. The World Resources Institute calculated the real cost of gas in 1991, when factoring in road construction, damages to our health and the environment, etc., to be close to $7 per gallon (who could afford to drive?). Seven dollars per gallon doesn't include the hidden subsidies the United States government is paying to support our auto-centric society in order for the dominant culture to gain financially from ever-increasing gas sales. The United States government pumps more money into subsidizing the use of automobiles than into Aid to Families with Dependent Children. Even excluding engagements such as Operation Desert Storm [the 1991 multinational war against Iraq], military expenditures to protect our foreign oil investments were estimated at between $15 billion and $54 billion in 1989.

Profiting from the high demand for fossil fuels that cars necessitate, oil companies will do almost anything in their power to get more petroleum, especially since three-quarters of all the extractable oil has already been extracted in the lower 48 states. *Survival International* reports that the American oil giant Mobil, the key member of a consortium which includes Elf and Exxon, is entering the territory of uncontacted Amazon Indians in Peru without their consent to undertake a massive oil exploration. Similar operations by Shell in the 1980's led to the deaths of between 50 and 100 Nahua Indians (more than half the population of the band they encountered) due to whooping cough and pneumonia. To what extent are we willing to go in order to sustain our auto-centric lifestyle? Are we willing to continue to consume fuel carelessly at the expense of the lives of innocent people? Reducing our use of cars and finding new modes of transportation will not only affect our society, but the world at large.

ALTERNATIVES TO FOSSIL FUELS

Yet, there are some situations where cars cannot be replaced so easily. In rural areas, for instance, where public transit is practically non-existent, the difference between owning a car and not owning a car is often employment or unemployment. Because distances are so great, we need transportation that will allow us to travel with speed and dependability. Also, those with disabilities have no choice but to use cars, especially when public transportation does not adequately answer their special needs. However, cars do not necessarily have to be powered by fossil fuel. Other forms of propulsion exist, such as electricity. The Sunrise by Solectria, a four-door passenger electric vehicle (EV) with the interior space of a Ford Taurus is expected to sell for around $20,000 in 1998. It traveled 238 miles in mixed city-highway driving before requiring a recharge (the average EV takes 6 hours to fully recharge using a 220 volt source). Another alternative is the hypercar. Propelled by four small electric motors, the hypercar uses fuel cells to generate electricity, which eliminates the use of large and heavy battery packs. With this configuration, the hypercar can exceed 200 miles per gallon of fuel (petroleum, natural gas, ethanol).

BIKING TO RAIL STATIONS

"Bike-and-ride" facilities, which encourage commuters to cycle to rail stations instead of drive, are increasingly popular in Japan and Western Europe. For years Japanese commuters have preferred bicycles over slow feeder buses for getting to suburban rail stations. Japan's 1980 census figures showed that 7.2 million commuters, or about 15 percent of the total, rode bicycles to work or to commuter rail stations. In Europe, the portion of railway passengers in suburbs and smaller towns who bicycle to the station varies from 10 to 55 percent. Stations often have spaces for hundreds of bicycles, and many public transport systems allow cyclists to bring their bikes on the bus or train.

Marcia D. Lowe, *Worldwatch Paper 98*, October 1990.

Although EVs and hypercars are much more efficient and less polluting than conventional automobiles, they still require important amounts of resources to manufacture; they are costly; and they depend on mega-infrastructures (power plants, highways, and parking space). I believe that we must limit our use of EVs or other less polluting vehicles to situations where sustainable means of transportation are not adequate, or where more personal means of transportation are not an option. Otherwise, we will only transform our current transportation problems into new ones.

The most subtle obstacles preventing the use of cleaner, safer, healthier, and cheaper means of transportation are the following deep-seated myths fabricated by car makers: the mystical bond between owner and car, the sense of freedom generated by owning a car, and the thrill of driving a car. If we are serious in encouraging people to let go of their gas-consuming cars and adopt more sustainable modes of transportation, we cannot ignore these emotional and spiritual dimensions. Fighting for the reduction of automobile use is not simply a matter of offering alternative ways of moving about. The greatest forms of public transportation will not replace the unquestioned belief that cars are a mystical extension of our being even though, while still tragic, only 20 bus passengers died in 1994, and a 10 percent increase in transit ridership in the five largest US cities would equal a savings of 85 million gallons of gasoline each year. Therefore, we must also offer sustainable means of transportation that will elicit true mystical experiences (oneness, freedom, and enjoyment), that will entice drivers away from their four-wheeled co-dependent companion.

The Human-Powered Vehicle Experience

What kind of transportation does not contribute to the massive destruction of the environment, improves physical and psychological health, is affordable to all, and elicits the experience of oneness, freedom, and pleasure? The answer is the most efficient and effective form of personal transportation ever conceived: the bicycle, or what many prefer to call a human-powered vehicle (HPV). HPVs require less energy to travel a given distance than any other form of personal transportation. (In contrast, only one percent of the total energy burned by conventional cars is spent on moving the driver's body and 15 percent on moving the car itself; the rest is wasted in heat.) There are definite drawbacks in riding an HPV: higher vulnerability to the elements, limited cargo space, and unfriendly motorists. But if we compare the many benefits of using an HPV with those of using a car, the drawbacks are well worth it, especially when HPVs are integrated with public transportation.

Ecological and Financial Benefits. Cycling is a non-polluting form of personalized transportation that neither consumes limited natural resources nor requires costly infrastructure to support. For every mile traveled by bicycle instead of by car, 2.6 grams of hydro-carbons, 20 grams of carbon monoxide, and 1.6 grams of nitrogen oxides are prevented from polluting the atmosphere. Bicycles can carry 1,500 persons per meter-width of lane per hour, compared with 750 persons by car. Moreover, it is available to nearly all segments of society for a fraction of the cost of a car (it is estimated that 100 bicycles can be produced from the materials required for an average-size car). There are very low maintenance costs, no fueling cost, no expensive insurance fees, and no parking fees.

Psychological and Social Benefits. HPVs also help reduce the fast pace of our auto-centric culture by reestablishing our natural rhythm of locomotion, a concept that has become foreign to our western mind in the past 50 years. Moving closer to our work, and giving ourselves more time to commute, can return us to a more human-paced and a less stressful lifestyle. Consequently, HPVs not only enhance our psychological well-being, but also revitalize our cities by encouraging people to live closer instead of farther away in dislocated suburbs. A necessary part of this revitalization is for local governments to spend less money on road construction and more on making car-free (pollution-free) areas in cities and towns (an idea that has been implemented in many European cities), which allows pedestrians and HPVs to travel safely and quietly in friendlier neighborhoods while breathing cleaner air.

FOR BODY, MIND, AND SOUL

Health and Medical Benefits. One of the greatest personal benefits of using an HPV is the return to the body. Unlike cars and public transportation, HPVs heighten our awareness of our bodies. As we respect our bodies as the organic engines they are, we learn to attend to their needs and functions. Proper diet, rest, and physical condition become part of our everyday concern, which considerably reduces health problems (people who exercise regularly have 41 percent fewer medical claims greater than $5,000). Healthy bodies are an integral part of a healthy society.

Spiritual Benefits: The Experience of Oneness. Cycling not only enhances the soul/body relationship, it also reconnects us with our surroundings. In the full enclosure of a car traveling at high speeds, our surroundings become inaccessible. It is comparable to seeing the world on television: it becomes something out there, instead of out here, a disconnected reality. Although some HPVs can travel at great speed (the current record is 65 mph), cycling allows us to experience our environment directly through sight, smell, touch, movement, and sound. As well as their new body awareness, many cyclists have described their close contact with their environment as mystical, flowing, wild, and ecstatic.

The Experience of Freedom. Promoting cars as a means to increase one's personal freedom ignores and contradicts the ever-growing headaches of actually owning them: mechanical failures, parking, insurance, car payments, break-ins, traffic jams, accidents, speeding tickets, and the list goes on. As for HPVs, these concerns are reduced to a minimum, which greatly simplifies life without seriously sacrificing our traveling independence. Letting go of things that hold too much space in our lives, such as cars, can set the stage for a spiritual deepening. "People must be so empty of all things and all works, whether inward or outward, that they can become a proper home for God, wherein God may operate," says Meister Eckhart, a 13th century mystic.

The Experience of Enjoyment. Another aspect that car manufacturers insist on reminding us again and again is how fun and exciting their vehicles are to drive. If this is true, why do so many people fall asleep or get stressed out while driving? Perhaps this is why car manufacturers need to keep convincing us how thrilling they are. As for HPVs, there is no need to spend millions in making us believe that they are fun to ride. Most people who use HPVs testify that they ride them because they enjoy doing it; and those riding recumbents (HPVs that enable the body to recline on a comfortable seat, have less wind drag than conventional bikes, and provide the cyclist with a much lower center of gravity) are convinced that there exists no other mode of transportation as exhilarating as recumbents. Engaging our body in physical activity, feeling the air brushing our face, experiencing firsthand the rushing speed, and sensing the challenge before us, all contribute to the joy of cycling. Moreover, there is a feeling of aliveness and of accomplishment that emerges within us, a state that often lasts long after the ride itself (and seldom happens when driving a car to work). In his book *The Age of Missing Information,* Bill McKibben describes the spiritual advantages of cycling when he writes:

> A bicycle is every bit as technological as an electric car, and as a significant minority of people have discovered, it's endlessly more elegant. On a bicycle you see the world around you—you notice the hills that a car obliterates; you see neighborhoods at a pace that makes them real, not a blur. You save gas, of course, but you also hear your body again.

Encouraging HPV Ridership

Publicizing the truth about the real cost of driving, educating the public on the many benefits of riding HPVs, and promoting the spiritual dimension of cycling can encourage many healthy commuters to switch from destructive and frustrating-to-drive cars to more efficient and playful-to-ride HPVs. However, without the adequate infrastructure (access to public transit, bike lanes, bike paths, and bike racks), encouraging people to bike to work continues to be a very difficult challenge. Nevertheless, if northern cities like Toronto, where one-fourth of all trips made by residents during peak hours are made by foot or bicycle, can put in place an infrastructure for the safer use of HPVs, then cities like Los Angeles, where winter is not a problem, can do even more. It is up to us to put pressure on our politicians to allocate more funds in building HPV infrastructure, and to provide incentives to use less polluting transportation.

Conscious or not, the type of transportation we use is a political statement. We need to ask ourselves, "Do I want to use a means of transportation that serves the self-interest of the corporate world and has no consideration for health, environment, psyche, or soul; or do I want to challenge the status quo and promote a more sustainable and spirit-filled mode of transportation?" What will it be?

> "Between its energy and non-energy
> uses, oil is the genie behind much of
> modern life."

OIL IS AN EFFICIENT ENERGY SOURCE

Lee R. Raymond

Lee R. Raymond is the chairman and CEO of Exxon Corporation. In the following viewpoint, a speech given at the Economic Club of Detroit on May 6, 1996, Raymond asserts that petroleum offers many benefits as an energy source and as an ingredient in products. Raymond contends that the abundance, affordability, and improved environmental impact of oil make it an attractive resource that will be needed to spur economic growth and provide energy into the future. He maintains that the petroleum industry is continuously discovering crude oil reserves and developing cleaner-burning fuels.

As you read, consider the following questions:

1. What did Americans associate oil with in the 1970s, according to Raymond?
2. What was the finding of the Princeton University study cited by Raymond?
3. On what basis does the author criticize government policy toward alternative fuels?

From Lee R. Raymond, "Energy, the Economy, and the Environment," a speech delivered May 6, 1996, to the Economic Club of Detroit, Detroit, Michigan. Reprinted by permission of the author.

We all know that Detroit is synonymous with the American automobile industry, and I would like to begin today by congratulating our friends in the auto industry on reaching their 100th anniversary. Of course, we in the petroleum industry have been fortunate to share much of the journey with you, and we have many ties. Both of our industries have a common set of customers. And it takes both of us to keep America and the world moving.

We've accomplished a great deal together. One very important environmental example is the progress we've made over the past quarter century in reducing vehicle emissions. With new technology from the auto industry and new fuels from the petroleum industry, we've reduced those emissions by 96 percent, and we'll make further progress in the years ahead. We believe that's a tremendous achievement, rarely acknowledged by our critics, and a source of pride for both industries.

Sustaining Economic Growth

The auto industry and the Economic Club of Detroit have another common bond with those of us in the petroleum industry. That is a strong interest in the need for economic growth and energy development while recognizing the impact on the environment.

Creating and sustaining economic growth is one of the great challenges facing the world. It is necessary to create more and better jobs, raise standards of living and provide hope for a brighter, more secure future for people around the world.

As I travel around the world, I see a different look on people's faces where economic growth is occurring. It's a look of excitement and optimism. And where it isn't occurring, the despair and resignation show that economic progress is more than numbers—it's a whole psychology of being.

The need for growth is universal, but it's especially strong in the developing nations. Those countries are where most of the world's population growth is occurring—growth which is expected to add 1.4 billion people to our planet by the year 2010. Developing nations are also where most of the world's poor people live. To meet the human needs in these countries, economic growth will be absolutely essential.

And to support economic growth, we need a second "E"— energy. Energy use and economic growth are inextricably linked. If you plot on a graph the countries with the highest standards of living, you will find that they are the countries with the highest energy use per capita. Today, most of that energy comes from fossil fuels—about 85 percent. Of these, oil and natural gas supply the majority, with oil alone supplying the lion's share, 40 percent of world energy demand. And we expect that to be true well into the future.

OIL'S PLACE IN THE WORLD

The predominant position of oil is understandable. Compared to other sources, it has a high energy density—that is, the amount of energy produced per unit of volume or weight. As a liquid fuel, it is very easy to transport and convenient to use. Contrary to current comments in the press, it is very affordable. And it is the most versatile energy source, used to run everything from cars, airplanes and ships to home furnaces, factories and electric power plants.

Oil also has many non-energy uses. In the petrochemical industry, it is used to create countless everyday products—from carpeting to clothing, detergents to disposable diapers, paints to video cassettes. The automobile itself is a rolling showcase for petrochemicals—used in everything from bumpers and dashboards to rubber hoses and tires, and even extending to the asphalt roads we drive on.

One might say as that between its energy and non-energy uses, oil is the genie behind much of modern life. But despite all the benefits, some people today are very concerned about oil. They see it as a finite resource whose use presents a grave danger to our environment. And they advocate very strong steps to curb its use.

This contemporary "petrophobia" contrasts sharply with the attitudes prevailing in the 1950s and '60s. Then, people tended to associate autos and oil with progress and the freedom of "Happy Motoring"—one of Exxon's ad slogans in those days.

The fear associated with oil has its most recent roots in the 1970s, and, in some ways, it is understandable. Twice during the 1970s, Middle East oil supplies were disrupted, leading to sharply higher price and price controls in this country that resulted in gasoline lines at service stations. Under such conditions, people in our country began to associate energy, especially oil, with loss of independence, limits on opportunity and another word—"crisis."

The environmental movement, which gained momentum in the 1970s, also played a role in changing the perception of oil. Critics in that movement faulted all fossil fuels, including oil, for their environmental impact. They pointed to renewable energy sources, such as solar, wind and geothermal, as alternatives to high-priced oil.

As we all know, in time, the energy crisis passed, oil prices dropped, and the industry developed cleaner oil-based products. But the negative perception of oil is still with us today.

As difficult as the challenges of the 1970s were, they should not blind us to the significant benefits derived from oil. Nor should they cause us to give in to fears about oil which its detractors raise. Let me briefly address the two major fears that are put forward—oil supply and environmental impact.

OIL RESERVES

Regarding supply, many people tend to see oil as a finite resource, but they forget that human ingenuity is not. Technological advances are adding greatly to our discovery and economic recovery of oil. And the result is that proved remaining world oil reserves actually grew by 40 percent between 1986 and 1996.

These reserves now represent a 45 year supply at current consumption, even if we never discover another barrel. But of course, we do find more oil all the time, and the long-term trend over the past several decades has been toward increasing, not diminishing, supplies of oil.

OIL PRICES PER BARREL, 1949–1993

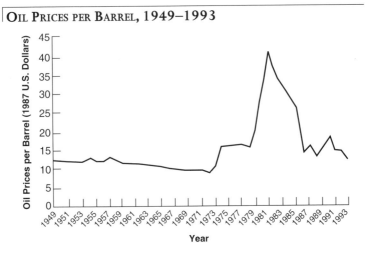

Source: Energy Information Administration, *Annual Energy Review 1993* (Washington, D.C.: U.S. Department of Energy, 1994).

The bulk of the current reserves—some two-thirds—are in the Middle East. But significant reserves also exist in other parts of the world—from the North Slope of Alaska to South America, from Africa to the North Sea. One very encouraging development is the doors that have opened since the collapse of communism. As a result of those changes, the area of the world open for energy development has been increased by more than one-third.

A few years ago, who would have thought companies such as Exxon would be exploring for petroleum and selling our products in China? Who would have thought we would be doing the same in Russia, Eastern Europe and Vietnam?

These new opportunities and the increasing economic interdependence of oil-producing and oil-importing countries have reduced the risk of oil supply disruptions. That fact was illustrated by the Persian Gulf War of 1991. Look at the alliance of nations involved. And notice the fact that, in marked contrast to the conflicts in that region in the 1970s, the most recent one did not result in any supply disruptions.

ENVIRONMENTAL PROGRESS

The other great fear about oil relates to the third "E"—environment. Some people believe that oil use is incompatible with a cleaner environment. But the truth is that we have made enormous progress over the past quarter century in reducing the environmental impact of oil and other fossil fuels and making them much cleaner to use.

Let me give you some data that illustrate the overall trend. In this country since 1970, lead emissions have decreased by 98 percent and breathable particulate matter by 78 percent. Sulfur dioxide emissions have dropped by more than 30 percent and are expected to be cut by some 40 percent more by the year 2000. Carbon monoxide has been cut by one quarter and is projected to be reduced by an additional 36 percent by the year 2000.

Like the auto industry, the petroleum industry has taken unprecedented steps to reduce the environmental impact of its products. Today, in the U.S. alone, the industry is spending at a rate of more than $10 billion per year on environmental improvement—as much as we spend searching for oil and gas in this country. Exxon itself spends some $2 billion per year worldwide on environmental measures.

During the past 20 years, the U.S. petroleum industry has introduced new, cleaner-burning motor fuels five times. Each of these new fuels has produced fewer pollutants than its predecessor. In 1995, we introduced reformulated gasoline that cuts summertime hydrocarbon emissions by 16 percent, with a 27 percent reduction projected when new standards take effect in the year 2000.

Unfortunately, many Americans are unaware of this progress. Public opinion surveys show that most Americans believe that the environment has actually gotten worse over the last two decades.

GLOBAL WARMING

Misunderstanding about environmental progress creates fertile ground for fear. Nowhere is that better illustrated than in the concerns expressed about global warming. The scientific evidence points to significant uncertainty around the issue. But you would not get that impression from the many news stories that appear on the subject.

Proponents of the global warming theory say that higher levels of greenhouse gases—especially carbon dioxide—are causing or will cause global temperatures to rise. But more than 96 percent of the carbon dioxide is naturally produced in the environment, and it has nothing to do with human activity. It, and the other greenhouse gases, are necessary for life to survive on earth. Currently, the scientific evidence is inconclusive as to whether human activities are having a significant effect on the global climate.

The lack of scientific understanding on this subject has not prevented activists from politicizing it and seeking to stir up all kinds of fears. They do so in an effort to force wrenching changes in our lifestyles and in the economies of the world's industrialized nations, with their real objectives often obscure. Such attempts represent a threat both to sound science and sound economics.

In the years ahead, most of the growth in carbon dioxide emissions will occur in the developing nations where the most pressing environmental problems are related to poverty, and not global climate change. According to the World Bank, one-third of the world's population is without adequate sanitation. More than one billion people are without safe drinking water. Millions of cases of disease are a direct result of the lack of these basic needs.

Addressing these problems will require economic growth, and that will necessitate increasing, not curtailing, the use of fossil fuels. This does not mean that we will inevitably experience grave consequences from global warming. We should keep in mind that some Cassandras of global warming were predicting the coming of a new ice age 20 years ago. And so, it makes little sense today to adopt economically punishing policies on the basis of uncertain predictions.

Our first priority ought to be to improve scientific understanding. Exxon is helping with that process by conducting its own research and by supporting that of others, including a major research effort at M.I.T. [Massachusetts Institute of Technology] on the science, economics and policy options of potential global warming.

There are other helpful steps we as a society can take that make sense in themselves, independent of the future findings of science on the issue. One is to encourage cost-effective energy efficiency programs so that we use all of our energy resources, including oil, as wisely as possible. Another is to promote sound forest management and reforestation policies, especially those that relate to the world's tropical rain forests.

Using energy wisely means applying it in a way that produces a net benefit for the economy and for the environment. Environmental extremists say we must make an either/or choice between economic and energy development on the one hand— and environmental protection on the other. My view is we need all three—and the history of the past 25 years in this country and in other developed nations around the world shows we can accomplish that.

Studies in the economic community support this idea. A study at Princeton found "no evidence that environmental quality deteriorates steadily with economic growth." Instead, they found that, after an initial phase of deterioration, economic growth brought environmental improvement. In most cases, the turning point occurs before a country reaches annual per capita income of about $12,000—about the level in Taiwan.

The truth is economic growth is needed to fund environmental improvement. And for that to take place, the world will need abundant, affordable and increasingly cleaner supplies of energy, and oil fills the bill.

OIL-BASED FUELS SURPASS ALTERNATIVES

Despite the recent upward spike in prices, gasoline, in real dollars, costs about half of what it did in 1950. And if you also consider gains in fuel efficiency, you find that the real cost of gasoline per mile driven has fallen by 70 percent since 1950.

As I mentioned earlier, oil-based fuels continue to get cleaner. Cleaner fuels and improved auto technology have allowed our country to reduce total annual automobile emissions by more than half since 1965—even though today there are twice as many cars on the road, driving twice as many miles.

Among the so-called alternative fuels, none measure up to oil in abundance, performance and affordability. For example, ethanol, which is made mainly from corn, is about as clean as reformulated gasoline, but costs twice as much to produce. That's, in part, because it takes about the same amount of energy to harvest, transport and process it as it yields as a fuel.

None of the alternative transportation fuels can take you as far as gasoline, as cheaply. Most of them have environmental issues of their own. And because they don't make good economic sense, the alternative fuels must be supported by government through subsidies or, in some cases, outright mandates.

We in the petroleum industry are not opposed to alternative fuels, and, as a matter of fact, Exxon itself is in a good position to benefit from supplying them. We need economically and environmentally attractive alternatives, and those that meet these criteria will succeed in a free marketplace. But government should not try to pick winners by subsidizing one alternative over the other or by specifically discriminating against oil-based products.

Unfortunately, that is taking place. Some federal and state legislation sets goals and mandates for alternative-fueled vehicles. Despite its excellent emissions performance, reformulated gasoline is not considered an alternative fuel in some states or under some laws, simply because it's made from oil.

The reason for this discrimination goes back to the fears I spoke of a moment ago—unfounded fears that result in ill-conceived laws and regulations. And so, the challenge for us in the petroleum industry is to do what I'm doing today—stand up in public and tell people that oil-based fuels are plentiful, affordable, clean and getting cleaner all the time.

In doing that, we look to natural allies such as the automobile industry for support. I recently heard an auto executive say that wherever he goes in the world, someone will come up and tell him that the internal combustion engine is an environmental villain whose time has passed. He says our industries are fighting a battle against misinformation, and I agree.

A SPIRIT OF COOPERATION

The internal combustion engine and the fuels that power it have greatly improved over the decades. We need to make that message clear to our mutual customers around the world. And we need to work together more closely on a range of other issues. We've cooperated in research programs on both sides of the Atlantic, and we need to continue and extend this cooperation.

A spirit of cooperation is also needed by society as a whole as we continue to solve environmental problems. I believe most thoughtful people would agree that we need to weigh costs and benefits and seek the most cost-effective solutions. Economic progress should not be put at risk to placate alarmists or ideologues. In promoting environmental improvements, we should rely more on free markets and less on government.

I do, however, see a key role for government to play in setting rational environmental standards and promoting policies that spur productive investment. But government should avoid the temptation to intervene in energy markets in ways that give an unfair advantage to one fuel over another. Government's goal should be to promote a fair contest on a level playing field.

This will allow all of society to move forward. And that's the message I would like to leave you with—the economy and energy, with careful consideration of the environment, moving forward together. If that happens, we can all look to economic growth, higher standards of living and hope for a brighter, more secure future for people all around the world.

PERIODICAL BIBLIOGRAPHY

The following articles have been selected to supplement the diverse views presented in this chapter. Addresses are provided for periodicals not indexed in the *Readers' Guide to Periodical Literature*, the *Alternative Press Index*, the *Social Sciences Index*, or the *Index to Legal Periodicals and Books*.

Drew Kodjak	"EVs: Clean Today, Cleaner Tomorrow," *Technology Review*, August/September 1996.
James J. MacKenzie	"Heading Off the Permanent Oil Crisis," *Issues in Science and Technology*, Summer 1996.
M. Miller	"Wind Industry News for the New Millennium," *Mother Earth News*, June/July 1996.
Ralph Nader	"Solar Powered Society Overdue," *Liberal Opinion Week*, August 12, 1996. Available from PO Box 468, Vinton, IA 52349.
Amal Kumar Naj	"You Can Buy Yourself an Electric Car, but It Isn't Going to Take You Very Far," *Wall Street Journal*, May 5, 1996.
New Internationalist	Special issue on energy, October 1996. Available from 1011 Bloor St. West, ON M6H 1M1, Canada.
Lawrence W. Reed	"The Electric Car Seduction," *Freeman*, November 1996. Available from Foundation for Economic Education, 30 S. Broadway, Irvington, NY 10533.
Daniel Sperling	"The Case for Electric Vehicles," *Scientific American*, November 1996.
William H. Timbers Jr.	"Betting on the Future of Nuclear Power," *Vital Speeches of the Day*, January 15, 1997.
James R. Udall	"Power to the People," *Sierra*, January/February 1997.
Bertram Wolfe	"Why Environmentalists Should Promote Nuclear Energy," *Issues in Science and Technology*, Summer 1996.

CHAPTER 4

HOW CAN GLOBAL RESOURCES BE PROTECTED?

CHAPTER PREFACE

"Sustainable development" is a catchphrase that frequently arises in discussions of global resources and the environment. Although the term has various meanings, sustainable development may be broadly defined as progress that meets the needs of today's generation without compromising the ability of future generations to meet their own needs. The concept rests on three pillars—economic growth, environmental protection, and social justice—and stresses maximum efficiency in the use of natural resources along with the protection of the livelihood of indigenous populations.

According to many environmental activists and others, governments can effectively lead citizens and industries along the path to sustainable development. As an example, they cite the Netherlands' National Environmental Policy Plan, "the best job of technical environmental planning done by any nation to date," according to Resource Renewal Institute founder Huey D. Johnson. Under its "green plan," the Dutch government aims to reduce the quantity of materials used by industries, double the lifespan of products, and ban the export of waste, among other goals.

However, other experts assert that government cannot match the power of the free market to protect global resources and the environment. According to Chicago geologist Richard Sanford, "What sustainable development really is is a smoke screen for socialism, where the government substitutes its will for that of the owner." Economists Jane S. Shaw and Richard L. Stroup oppose environmental regulations "because government policies often subsidize wasteful activities and can lead to environmental degradation." They add that "the road to sustainable development is to let the [market] forces that have worked well continue to work."

Whether the free market and economic growth can effectively protect global resources and encourage sustainable development is examined by the authors in this chapter.

| "Economic growth plays [a vital role] in the progress toward environmental quality."

ECONOMIC GROWTH CAN PROTECT GLOBAL RESOURCES

Earnie Deavenport

Earnie Deavenport is the chairman and CEO of Eastman Chemical Co. in Kingsport, Tennessee. In the following viewpoint, Deavenport argues that in order to protect global resources and maintain environmental quality, governments should encourage economic growth through free markets. Deavenport contends that societies in which free markets are allowed to operate experience high rates of economic growth, resulting in the development of industrial technologies that are less environmentally destructive and wasteful. Therefore, Deavenport insists, free enterprise is more effective than government regulations at protecting the world's resources.

As you read, consider the following questions:

1. According to the World Bank, cited by Deavenport, what is the income threshold at which a society chooses to improve the environment?
2. How do international environmental protection conventions affect economic growth, according to the author?
3. In Deavenport's opinion, what must an international environmental regulatory system encourage?

From Earnie Deavenport, "Standing at the Edge of History," a speech delivered at the Fourth Forum of the World Chemical Industries, Paris, France, April 25, 1996. Reprinted by permission of the author.

Let me set the stage for my talk today with a phrase coined by the American economist Barbara Ward nearly 25 years ago.

She was concerned that the biosphere of our inheritance and the technosphere of our creation were out of balance, and that the door of the future was opening onto a crisis unlike any other we had ever experienced. As a result, she said, we were standing at "the hinge of history."

The actions we take now in support of the concept of sustainable development—at this "hinge of history"—have the potential to generate change on a global scale for the benefit—or detriment—of all life on earth.

As nations around the word come together to more fully focus on the economic, environmental, and social legacy our generation leaves on this earth for future generations, I believe, now more than ever, that good environmental policy hinges on good business policy.

If history has taught us anything, it is that environmental performance and economic performance work best when they work together. The record shows that our industry can do more good for the world economy, more good for the global environment, and more good for the social welfare of people everywhere if it is allowed to fully utilize its scientific principles, its ability to prioritize risks, and its ability to make value judgments based on objective cost-benefit analysis.

COST-EFFECTIVE RISK MANAGEMENT

Simply put, the key to sustainable development is cost-effective risk management, and that is what I want to talk about today.

But first, let me explain the principle of cost-effective risk management.

The role of risk and how to manage risk are the focal points in the current struggle to reform and remake the environmental regulatory framework in the United States.

The U.S. chemical industry championed the use of risk management and its key elements of risk assessment, risk prioritization, cost-benefit analysis, and peer review of scientific data as a way of improving the U.S. environment and increasing its standard of living through a strong economy.

We view the principle of risk management as a common sense process for allocating scarce financial, human, and natural resources to activities that can provide the most benefit at the least cost to society.

We are also firm in our belief that we have a moral obligation to future generations to protect and use our limited resources wisely. Without such an obligation, the goal of sustainable development cannot be achieved.

Although we today cannot define the needs of tomorrow's generations, we can work together to make certain that future generations are not limited in their choices when it comes their time to forge their own destiny.

Choices leading to a healthy environment and social equity will be theirs for the making if our generation will commit to the principle of cost-effective risk management and obligate itself to a strong world economy.

A Change in Attitude

And we are making great progress. For more than 25 years now, industries worldwide have been going through a generational change in attitude toward the environment. Environmental ethics are now an integral part of our business strategies, and we have developed cleaner, energy-efficient processes that manufacture products that are healthier, safer, and more environmentally responsible.

In the U.S., we have now reached the point with this shift in attitude that leading-edge environmental technology no longer resides with government, but resides now with the business community.

Out of this change is emerging a new and modem environmental model.

This new model is replacing the old U.S. "command and control" model because society is recognizing that industry, with its advanced technologies, can provide a cleaner environment at a lower cost than government can provide.

Unlike the command and control model, this new model is based on the fact that, when individual consumers are provided with truthful and accurate information in an open and free marketplace, they will make an educated and moral choice that will simultaneously lead to economic prosperity, environmental improvement, and social equity.

This emerging model is also based on the principles of risk management that, when applied in a free market, lead to economic efficiencies, which in turn lead to an improved environment and an ever increasing standard of living.

Studies show that as a nation becomes more economically efficient through industrial specialization and open trade, per capita income increases. And as personal income increases, environmental quality and social well-being improve. According to the World Bank, an annual per capita income of $5,000 is the threshold at which a society will choose to make environmental improvements, and usually does.

A Cleaner Tokyo

Perhaps you have witnessed, as I have, examples that bear this out.

Back in the mid-60's, I visited Tokyo for the very first time. It was a lot bigger, a lot more crowded, and a whole lot more polluted than I ever expected. Today, Tokyo is still a big, crowded city, but it has one remarkable difference. Of all the major world cities I occasionally visit, Tokyo is now my favorite because it is so environmentally clean.

The major reason for Tokyo's environmental transformation, I believe, is an increase in Japan's per capita income. Back in the mid-60's, Japan's per capita income was in the neighborhood of $6,000 a year, just above the World Bank threshold. Today, it's over $21,000.

I recently made a world tour as a guest of *Time* magazine that included visits to Havana, Moscow, Hanoi, Bangalore, India and several other hot spots. On that tour I witnessed firsthand that environmental quality hinges on a sound economy.

Environmental Improvement Depends on Economic Progress

In the twenty-first century it will be clear that the preservation of natural resources and the expansion of human ones are tightly linked. This concept may be very hard for traditionalists to accept, but history has shown that environmental improvement depends directly on rapid economic progress. If poor countries do not adopt modern high-yield agriculture, for example, then their impoverished farmers will be forced by hunger to level millions of square miles of wildlands.

Ronald Bailey, *The True State of the Planet*, 1995.

I saw these once great cities in decline, their nation's economic potential being squandered, their local environment being slowly and methodically stripped of its natural resources, and their populations subjected to abject poverty. All because their governments are still waiting to recognize the power of the free market and the potential of cost-effective risk management.

That tour confirmed for me, more than anything in my life, that when too much responsibility is shifted to government, individual freedom to make a responsible choice in a free market is reduced at the expense of the environment.

When the OECD [Organization for Economic Cooperation and Development] Environmental Ministers met in Paris in 1996, there was concern that the rapid globalization now taking place throughout the world might have a detrimental effect on the world environment.

Those of us on the front lines of this globalization effort find comfort in the knowledge that our industry, with its development and transfer of clean technologies, is doing more to improve the environment by establishing economic stability and peace than ever before in industrial history.

The chemical industries in 40 countries have voluntarily developed long-term plans to integrate environmental performance with economic activity through a worldwide initiative we call Responsible Care.

Recycling, waste minimization, and product stewardship have now become an integral part of our business code of conduct because these responsible environmental activities make good economic and social sense.

ECONOMIC GROWTH FOR SUSTAINABLE DEVELOPMENT

In a published report to President Bill Clinton, the President's Council on Sustainable Development officially acknowledges the vital role that economic growth plays in the progress toward environmental quality. It is comforting to know that the President's council recognizes the role of a strong economy in achieving sustainable development.

However, the reality is that our industry, as a major player in the world economy, is threatened by a series of existing and potential international conventions that limit our ability to contribute to a strong global economy, thereby rolling back sustainable development.

Under the current concept of sustainable development, there is a broad-based drive to stagnate industry in order to control consumption. This approach to improving the environment by impairing industrial activity is misguided and will eventually do the environment more harm than good.

Supposedly, exceptions would be made for environmental technology. But this centralized form of decision-making can have perverse and contradicting results.

Here is a case in point. The President's Council on Sustainable Development proposed, as a pilot project, to create a new form of development called eco-industrial parks. This new form of development follows a system of design in which one facility's waste becomes another facility's feedstock.

If this concept of development is believed to be workable in our local villages, is it not reasonable to believe that such a development system should work in our global village as well?

If so, why are international conventions, such as the Basel Convention [an agreement to ban many exports of hazardous wastes to developing countries], driven to stop open trade between developed and developing nations in such valuable materials as scrap metals? Conventions like these virtually eliminate the power of choice in a free market and impede sustainable development by retarding the progress of increasing per capita income.

In a speech at Harvard University, [then-]U.S. Secretary of State Warren Christopher announced the unprecedented move to fully integrate U.S. environmental goals into international diplomacy. This further intrusion by government could be a detriment to the advancement of sustainable development by diminishing the power of the free market and open trade.

If the concept of sustainable development is to become a reality, we must work together to build an international regulatory system that encourages industry to voluntarily change its behavior. Instead, we are forced to react to prescriptive international conventions that stifle innovation, institutionalize misinformation, and perpetuate command and control.

The best way to save our planet is to save the people on it from poor sanitation, dirty drinking water, and from using "age old" farming techniques that deplete the land, hasten deforestation, and promote soil erosion.

I call upon environmentalists everywhere, who really want to improve the global environment, to join me and my industrial colleagues in eradicating poverty, improving literacy rates, and elevating educational standards.

FULL PARTICIPATION

These are life-long, sustaining fundamentals that provide for a wider bottom-up, rather than a narrow top-down, participation in risk management. Only through full participation will the goal of sustainable development be achieved.

[Former Indian prime minister] Indira Ghandi said, "A nation's strength ultimately consists in what it can do on its own, and not in what it can borrow from others."

Strong national economies based on the principle of cost-effective risk management is the key.

Governments can play an important role by demanding truth in advertising and by assuring that quality and relevant information is available for making individual moral choices.

In closing, risk management must be considered by national and local governments, as well as by international organizations, as a vehicle for emphasizing the role of a strong economy in achieving the goal of sustainable development.

The message for all of us is that we should not merely settle for those actions that promise an easy path to the future.

It would be far easier for us all to simply accept the current economic, environmental, and social situation for what it is, and continue to travel along a path in which the promise of sustainable development will always be just beyond our reach.

A giant of our time, Charles de Gaulle [French president from 1958 to 1969], once said that France was never its true self except when it has engaged in a great enterprise. I believe that the same is true of companies and individuals. I believe it's certainly true of the concerned and dedicated men and women of the chemical industry worldwide.

Our great enterprise is a healthy environment for our small planet. If we pursue the right course at this hinge of history—a course of cost-effective risk management—I have no doubt that the door of the future will open onto great promise and opportunity for generations to come.

|"Overcrowded cities, unusual new
weather patterns, . . . the destruction
of wilderness, even the disappearance
of songbirds—are the products of
the same global policies."

ECONOMIC GROWTH CANNOT
PROTECT GLOBAL RESOURCES

Jerry Mander

In the following viewpoint, Jerry Mander argues that a global-ized free-market economy will fail to protect global resources and will endanger the environment. Mander contends that components of a global economy—free trade, increased consumption, and the elimination of regulatory controls—threaten to wreak havoc in nature and among human beings in the form of resource depletion, species loss, maximum levels of pollution, and increased poverty. Mander is the coeditor of *The Case Against the Global Economy*, from which this viewpoint is excerpted.

As you read, consider the following questions:
1. What does Mander mean by "monoculture"?
2. In Mander's opinion, what have the mass media failed to do?
3. What effect did the North American Free Trade Agreement have in Mexico, according to the author?

From Jerry Mander, "Corporate Colonialism," *Resurgence*, November/December 1996, which was adapted from "Facing the Rising Tide" by Jerry Mander, in *The Case Against the Global Economy*, edited by Jerry Mander and Edward Goldsmith. Copyright ©1996 by Jerry Mander and Edward Goldsmith. Reprinted with permission of Sierra Club Books.

Economic globalization involves arguably the most funda-mental re-design of the planet's political and economic ar-rangements since at least the Industrial Revolution. Yet the pro-found implications of these fundamental changes have barely been exposed to serious public scrutiny or debate. Despite the scale of the global reordering, neither our elected officials nor our educational institutions nor the mass media have made a credible effort to describe what is being formulated or to ex-plain its root philosophies.

The occasional descriptions or predictions about the global economy that *are* found in the media usually come from the leading advocates and beneficiaries of this new order: corporate leaders, their allies in government, and a newly powerful cen-tralized global trade bureaucracy. The visions they offer us are unfailingly positive, even utopian: Globalization will be a panacea for our ills.

BREAKDOWNS IN SOCIETY AND NATURE

Shockingly enough, the euphoria they express is based on their freedom to deploy, at a global level—through the new global free-trade rules, and through deregulation and economic re-structuring regimes—large-scale versions of the economic theo-ries, strategies and policies that have proven spectacularly unsuc-cessful over the past several decades wherever they've been applied. In fact, these are the very ideas that have brought us to the grim situation of the moment: the spreading disintegration of the social order and the increase of poverty, landlessness, homelessness, violence, alienation and, deep within the hearts of many people, extreme anxiety about the future. Equally im-portant, these are the practices that have led us to the near breakdown of the natural world, as evidenced by such symp-toms as global climate change, ozone depletion, massive species loss, and near maximum levels of air, soil and water pollution.

We are now being asked to believe that the development pro-cesses that have further impoverished people and devastated the planet will lead to diametrically different and highly beneficial outcomes, if only they can be accelerated and applied every-where, freely, without restriction: that is, when they are *globalized*.

That's the bad news. The good news is that it is not too late to stop this from happening.

A GLOBAL ECONOMIC ORDER

The passage of the Uruguay Round of GATT (the General Agree-ment on Tariffs and Trade) with its associated WTO (World Trade

Organization) was celebrated by the world's political leadership and transnational corporations as a sort of global messianic rebirth. They claim that these new arrangements will bring on a global economic order that can produce a $250 billion expansion of world economic activity in a very short time, with the benefits "trickling down" to us all. The dominant political-economic homily is "the new rising tide will lift all boats."

THE GREEN WAVE VS. FREE TRADE

There are now two major but contradictory trends in the world—the Green Wave and Free Trade. The "Green Wave" is the result of a rapidly growing realization by both the public and governments that the unchecked operations of companies and the economy are causing environmental and health catastrophes.

Around the world, legislatures are increasingly acting to control the destructive operations of corporations, economic projects and industrial plants. There is increasing awareness of corporate crimes (including insider trading, financial fraud, the falsification of safety tests, the knowing sale of toxic products and the illegal dumping of wastes) and the need to tighten controls to prevent such corporate abuses.

Against the Green Wave's call for more effective regulation of companies, there has emerged a powerful counter-trend that advocates the granting of unhampered freedom for "market forces" to dominate economic and other spheres of life.

Under the banner of "free market," "free trade," "deregulation," "privatization" and "liberalization," this trend calls for maximizing corporate access to resources while minimizing the role of governments to participate in economic activity or to regulate the behavior and effects of the companies. This battle for the "free market" started at the national level but now corporations hope to extend their economic reach to the international level under the guise of "free trade."

Martin Khor Kok Peng, *Earth Island Journal*, Summer 1992.

Indeed, the global economy is new, but less so in form than in scale: the new global rules by which it now operates; the technologically enhanced speedup of global development and commerce that it facilitates; and the abrupt shift in global political power that it introduces. Surely it is also new that the world's democratic countries voted to suppress their own democratically enacted laws in order to conform to the rules of the new central global bureaucracy. Also new is the elimination of most regulatory control over global corporate activity and the liberation of currency from national controls, which lead in turn to the *casino economy*, ruled by currency speculators.

But the deep ideological principles underlying the global economy are not so new: they are the very principles that have brought us to the social, economic and environmental impasse we are in. They include the primacy of economic growth; the need for free trade to stimulate the growth; the unrestricted "free market"; the absence of government regulation; and voracious consumerism combined with an aggressive advocacy of a uniform worldwide development model that faithfully reflects the Western corporate vision and serves corporate interests. The principles also include the idea that all countries—even those whose cultures have been as diverse as, say, Indonesia, Japan, Kenya, Sweden and Brazil—must sign on to the same global economic model and row their (rising) boats in unison. The net result *is monoculture*—the global homogenization of culture, lifestyle, and level of technological immersion, with the corresponding dismantling of local traditions and economies. Soon, everyplace will look and feel like everyplace else, with the same restaurants and hotels, the same clothes, the same malls and superstores, and the same streets crowded with cars. There'll be scarcely a reason ever to leave home.

ECOLOGICAL UNCERTAINTY

Globalization of the economy is a new kind of corporate colonialism, visited upon poor countries and the poor in rich countries.

But does this system work? Will the promised economic expansion of GATT actually happen? If so, can it sustain itself? Where will the resources—the energy, the wood, the minerals, the water—come from to feed the increased growth? Where will the effluents of the process—the solids and the toxics—be dumped? Who benefits from this? Who will benefit most? Will it be working people, who seem to be losing jobs to machines and corporate flight? Will it be farmers who, thus far, whether in Asia, Africa or North America, are being manoeuvred off their lands to make way for huge corporate monocultural farming— no longer producing diverse food products for local consumption but coffee and beef for export markets with their declining prices? Will it be city dwellers, now faced with the immigrant waves of newly landless peoples desperate to find the rare and poorly paid job?

And what of the ecological results? Can ever-increasing consumption be sustained forever? When will the forests be gone? How many cars can be built and bought? How many roads can

cover the land? What will become of the animals and the birds—
does anyone care about that? Is life better from this? Is all the destruction worth the result? Are we, as individuals, as families,
and as communities and nations, made more secure, less anx-
ious, more in control of our destinies? Can we possibly benefit
from a system that destroys local and regional governments
while handing real power to faceless corporate bureaucracies in
Geneva, Tokyo and Brussels? Will people's needs be better served
from this? Is it a good idea or a bad one? Do we want it? If not,
how do we reverse the process?

A RAVAGED PLANET

The German economic philosopher Wolfgang Sachs argues in
his book *The Development Dictionary* that the only thing worse than
the failure of this massive global development experiment
would be its success. For, even at its optimum performance
level, the long-term benefits go only to a tiny minority of people who sit at the hub of the process and to a slightly larger minority that can retain an economic connection to it, while the
rest of humanity is left groping for fewer jobs and less land, living in violent societies on a ravaged planet. The only boats that
will be lifted are those of the owners and managers of the process; the rest of us will be on the beach, facing the rising tide.

Our society has been massively launched onto a path to we-
know-not-where, and the people in the media who are supposed
to shed light on events that affect us have neglected to do so.

From time to time, the mass media do report on some major
problem of globalization, but the reporting rarely conveys the
connections between the specific crises they describe and the
root causes in globalization itself. In the area of environment,
for example, we read of changes in global climate and occasionally of their long-term consequences, such as the melting polar
ice caps, the expected staggering impacts to agriculture and food
supply, or the destruction of habitat. We read too of the ozone
layer depletion, the pollution of the oceans, or the wars over resources such as oil and, perhaps soon, water. But few of these
matters are linked directly to the imperatives of global economic
expansion, the increase of global transport, the overuse of raw
materials, or the commodity-intensive lifestyle that corporations
are selling worldwide via the culturally homogenizing technology of television and its parent, advertising. Obfuscation is the
net result.

Some publications have carried stories about "corporate
greed" as expressed by the firing of thousands of workers while

corporate profits soared and top executive salaries were being raised to unheard-of levels. Even these stories, however, rarely mentioned the crucial point that the new corporate restructuring is directly hooked to the imperatives of globalization and that it is happening all over the world. Obfuscation yet again.

In the autumn of 1995, the international press carried reports on the paralyzing strike by hundreds of thousands of French railway and other public service workers. Most reports characterized the workers as trying to protect their privileges, benefits and jobs against government cutbacks. True enough. But most stories left out that the cutbacks were mandated by the rules of Europe's Maastricht "single currency" agreement, itself part of the corporatizing, homogenizing and globalizing of Europe's economic system to make it compatible and competitive globally.

HARM TO INDIGENOUS LANDS

The media also report daily about the immigration crises, about masses of people trying to cross borders in search of jobs, only to be greeted by xenophobia, violence, and demagoguery in high places. But the role that international trade agreements play in making life impossible for people in their countries of origin is not visible in such reports. The North American Free Trade Agreement (NAFTA), for example, was a virtual knockout blow to the largely self-sufficient, small, corn-farming economy of Mexico's indigenous peoples—as the Zapatista rebels tried to illuminate in 1994—making indigenous lands vulnerable to corporate buyouts and foreign competition from the United States. Meanwhile, in India, Africa and South America, similar World Bank development schemes over the past few decades have deliberately displaced whole populations of relatively prosperous peoples, including small-scale self-sufficient farmers, to make way for giant dams and other megadevelopment schemes. The result of such "development" is that millions of small farmers are turned into landless refugees seeking nonexistent urban jobs.

Now and then we see media reports on food shortages, yet rarely is the connection drawn between hunger and the increased control of the world's food supply by a small number of giant (subsidized) corporations, notably Cargill, which effectively determines where food will grow, under which conditions it will grow and what ultimate price consumers will pay. The food, rather than being eaten by local people who grow it, is now typically shipped thousands of miles (at great environmental cost) to be eaten by the already well fed.

Horrible new disease outbreaks are very thoroughly reported

with ghoulish relish in the Western press. The part that is omitted, however, is the connection between these outbreaks and the destruction of rainforest and other habitats. As economic expansionism proceeds, previously uncontacted organisms hitch rides on new vectors for new territory.

We also read stories about the "last indigenous tribes" in the Amazon, Borneo, Africa or the Philippines; stories that lament the inevitability that native people, even against their clearly articulated wishes, even against the resistance of arrows and spears, must be drawn into the Western economic model to benefit from our development plans. Insufficiently reported are the root causes of this: the demands of economic growth for more water or forest resources; the desperate need for new lands for beef cattle, coffee or timber plantations; the equally desperate need to convert previously self-sufficient peoples into consumer clones. This is not to mention the far deeper need to destroy the "other" for the psychological threat they represent and for their example of viability in an entirely alternative context.

EFFECTS OF TECHNOLOGY

As for the role of technology, the powers that be continue to speak of each new generation of technological innovation in the same utopian terms they used to describe each preceding generation, going back to the private automobile; plastics and "clean nuclear energy," each introduced as panaceas for society. Now we have global computer networks that are said to "empower" communities and individuals, when the exact opposite is the case. The global computer-satellite linkup, besides offering a spectacular new tool for financial speculation, empowers the global corporation's ability to keep its thousand-armed global enterprise in constant touch, making instantaneous adjustments at the striking of a key. Computer technology may actually be the most centralizing technology ever invented, at least in terms of economic and political power. This much is certain: The global corporation of today could not exist without computers. The technology makes globalization possible by conferring a degree of control beyond anything ever seen before.

Meanwhile, new technologies such as biotechnology bring the development framework to entirely new terrain by enabling the enclosure and commercialization of the internal wilderness of the gene structure, the building blocks of life itself. The invention and patenting of new life forms, from cells to insects to animals to humans, will have profound effects on Third World agriculture, ecology and human rights.

WHAT GLOBAL DEVELOPMENT BRINGS

The point is this: all of the subjects are treated by the media, government officials and corporations alike as if they were totally unrelated. This is not helpful to an insecure public that is attempting to grasp what's happening and what might be done about it. The media do not help us to understand that each of these issues—overcrowded cities, unusual new weather patterns, the growth of global poverty, the lowering of wages while stock prices soar, the elimination of local social services, the destruction of wilderness, even the disappearance of songbirds—are the products of the same global policies. They are all of one piece, a fabric of connections that are ecological, social and political in nature. They are reactions to the world's economic-political restructuring in the name of accelerated global development. This restructuring has been designed by economists and corporations and encouraged by subservient governments; soon it will be made mandatory by international bureaucrats, who are beyond democratic control.

"Companies have excelled beyond
regulatory compliance . . . to entirely
redesign their products and services
to be more sustainable."

COMPANIES ARE INCREASINGLY PROTECTING GLOBAL RESOURCES

Sue Hall

In the following viewpoint, Sue Hall argues that proactive companies in many different industries are embracing procedures that protect natural resources and the environment. According to Hall, companies that restructure themselves to produce more sustainable products are winning a greater market share for these products. She maintains that companies that continue to cause environmental problems will become uncompetitive. Hall is the executive director of the Institute for Sustainable Technology in Underwood, Washington.

As you read, consider the following questions:

1. In Hall's opinion, what choices do companies face regarding how they operate?
2. According to the author, how were Shaman's pharmaceutical drugs developed?
3. What spurred increases in the sale of Arm & Hammer's baking soda, according to Hall?

During the celebrations of Earth Day 1990, I found myself repeatedly asking a simple question. Could companies gain competitive advantage from becoming environmental leaders?

There was much noise and celebration surrounding corporations' contributions to the environment. Lots of talk about pollution prevention, and the million dollar savings that 3M had generated from its total quality environmental programs. More intriguing, to my mind, were some of the companies which had begun to mount more proactive, innovative initiatives. Wellman, for example, had linked up with Pepsi and Coke bottlers to produce recycled PET [polyethylene teraphthalite] plastic, while Shaman Pharmaceuticals was researching potential new drugs by learning from traditional indigenous healers.

Was the marketplace rewarding companies that had begun to mount more proactive environmental initiatives? If so, we might be able to more deeply harness the power of the marketplace to serve and support sustainability.

So began five years of research and consulting designed to explore this question. In every industry I have investigated to date, I have found at least one company successfully "leading the change" toward more sustainable practices to produce significant competitive advantage. These companies have excelled beyond regulatory compliance, beyond the cost-saving achievements of pollution prevention, to entirely redesign their products and services to be more sustainable. Some have even changed their industries' rules of the game, forcing their competitors to adopt similarly sustainable practices.

These proactive companies were more successful because they were willing to respond early to signals that the market was restructuring in response to environmental challenges and were prepared to partner with, rather than oppose, environmental stakeholders to co-create solutions to tackle these issues. Having now researched dozens of industries and interviewed as many companies to understand why such leadership has been rewarded competitively, the following picture has emerged.

MARKET RESTRUCTURING: A GATEWAY TO SUSTAINABILITY

What all of these leading companies recognized is that environmental forces were beginning to restructure their marketplaces. These environmental forces were causing whole product markets to go into serious decline, while creating others to grow dramatically in their place. For example, as lead was phased out of gasoline, sales of tetraethyl lead declined to virtually zero by the early 1990s. By contrast, sales of MTBE [methyl tertiary butyl ether], a safer anti-knock replacement, were rising dramatically. Sales of HCFCs [hydrochlorofluorocarbons] had similarly expanded to replace CFCs until they too declined in the face of further environmental opposition.

Across a broad array of markets downstream of the chemicals industry—including pulp and paper, detergents, solvents, and gasoline—the same trend could be seen. Chemicals like chlorine or phosphates that were causing major environmental problems in downstream markets were suffering serious decline. By contrast, chemicals that were helping to solve those same problems were enjoying exceptionally rapid growth.

PRODUCT-LIFE EXTENSION

In some countries, the very nature of a "product" is challenged. The Swiss and Germans are pioneering "product-life extension" industrial policies, in which the *use* of a product is sold, rather than the product itself. A company gets its profits from continuing stewardship of the things they make and through service to the user. Agfa-Gevaert has adopted this approach with its copiers; the German auto makers are moving in this direction. The products are designed to last, to be maintained, improved, and disassembled for reuse rather than bought and dumped. Business itself can then de-materialize into more and more service functions, giving further hope that "industry" and "ecology" might co-exist after all.

Elizabeth Pinchot, In Context, Summer 1995.

Similarly, in the oil industry, companies like Chevron were mounting serious efforts to improve their environmental and social performance to gain a share of the lucrative oil exploration market by becoming the operator-of-choice in environmentally sensitive regions. Meanwhile, downstream, oil was losing its share of the energy market to natural gas, which has much lower emissions of SOx [sulfur oxides], NOx [nitrogen oxides], and CO_2 [carbon dioxide] per unit of energy.

These examples suggested that environmental concerns were beginning to seriously restructure entire marketplaces, up and down the value chain. Environmental challenges were becoming more than regulatory issues for business. They were beginning to create profoundly market-based challenges and opportunities.

A SIMPLE CHOICE

I would argue that this market restructuring poses a rather stark choice to companies. They can choose to deny this reality and continue with business as usual, rather than innovating to create more sustainable products and services. In this case, their businesses will continue to cause environmental problems, fueling the market restructuring and ultimately creating a downward competitive spiral for the company.

By contrast, a company can decide to learn from other stakeholders—such as environmental groups, regulators, the media, and so forth—in order to create more sustainable products for its core businesses. This decision further fuels the market restructuring, but this time to the company's advantage. The creation of these "green" products in turn helps to accelerate the pace of the environmental market restructuring, creating new competitive rules of the game from which these leading companies are uniquely well positioned to benefit.

THE LAGGARDS' VIEW

However, most companies do not recognize the potential of this environmental market restructuring. When we surveyed the US chemicals industry, we found that managers saw only 9 percent of their environmental challenges arising in downstream markets which were restructuring and creating major declines and growth in their product sales. Similarly, less than 8 percent of environmental challenges were seen to be arising in upstream markets—where companies like Chevron were seeking to gain market share by becoming the environmental operator of choice.

Although most companies' policies (63 percent) focus on compliance concerns, by contrast, their executives felt that 25 percent of future opportunities lay in new business lines that environmental issues were creating in downstream markets. A sea-change was in the air, which some companies had begun to sense and capitalize upon.

THE LEADERS' VIEW

Leading companies have clearly gained competitive advantage by recognizing and responding to this environmental market restructuring. Spanning over a dozen industries, these companies have gained market share, increased profit margins, or entirely changed the competitive rules of the game to create incremental value for themselves—and for the environment—as a result of their response to these environmental forces.

Take Henkel, for example, one of Europe's largest chemicals and detergents companies. In the late 1970s, Henkel began to notice the concerns rising in West Germany surrounding the potential impact of phosphates in detergents on rivers and streams. At the time, Henkel manufactured 50 percent of the country's phosphates and sold 49 percent of its phosphate-based detergents.

Instead of attempting to downplay the problem, Henkel decided to invest considerable R&D [research and development] monies into finding a substitute for phosphates. The company's success led to the surprising and courageous decision to cannibalize both of its phosphates businesses—up- and downstream— and replace them with new products based upon their patented substitute, *zeolite*.

Henkel was the first consumer products company to introduce phosphate-free detergents in Europe, entirely replacing all their old product lines. As a result, the company increased its market share from 16 percent to 23 percent for its top brand in Germany, and strengthened its foothold in the French market, gaining a 6 percent share for its phosphate-free brand. At the same time, Henkel, in conjunction with joint venture partner Degussa, built a 70 percent market share of the European zeolite production capacity, while its former phosphate production competitors were suffering major overcapacity and hemorrhaging losses.

GASOLINE, PLASTICS, AND PHARMACEUTICALS

Similarly hopeful examples can be found in industries as improbable as oil and gas. When Arco first noticed the likely shift towards lead-free gasoline, it moved early into MTBE, ending up with the largest worldwide share of this expanding market. More surprisingly still, Arco led its industry again with a decision, in August 1991, to replace all of its leaded gasoline sales in California with a new reformulated product, EC^1. EC^1 is a specially designed substitute formulated to run on pre-1975 cars, which accounted for only 15 percent of gasoline sales but 30 percent of the California auto pollution problem. Arco's market share rose dramatically from under 17 percent to over 25 percent in just nine months.

Leaders can even be found in industries as notorious as plastics. Wellman, for example, sustained a 40 percent growth rate and 21 percent return on equity over a period of six years when, almost a decade ahead of other plastics companies, it took on the challenge of creating the market for the recycled plastic, PET. Wellman teamed up with a set of non-traditional allies, including Coke and Pepsi bottlers who were recovering their used PET bottles from the bottle-bill states. This leadership helped PET become one of the most heavily recycled plastics—which in turn enabled PET to gain market share over rival resins, enhancing Wellman's sales still further.

As competitors began to invade Wellman's niche, it expanded its recycled product range downstream into the fibers business, helping to catalyze yet another high-value recycled materials market by selling these Coke and Pepsi bottles to Patagonia to manufacture a new line of "recycled" fleecy outdoor clothing.

Other companies have begun to change the rules of the game in their industries. Shaman was formed in 1990 to develop pharmaceutical drugs by learning from traditional indigenous healers [and the] plants they use to treat various diseases. When these plants are tested for effectiveness in treating those diseases, half the plants test positive—a hit rate over 50 times that of most drug companies.

Two Shaman drugs may complete their FDA [Food and Drug Administration] trials within 7–8 years of their initial plant screening, compared to an average of 10–12 years for conventional drug companies. Since the FDA grants patent protection—and thus exclusive "monopoly" profits—to drug companies for up to 17 years after initial screening, this could provide Shaman with up to 4 years' additional protected revenues and profits.

Shaman plans to share the profits from these potentially billion-dollar drugs with the indigenous communities from whom it first learned of such possibilities—offering an alternative revenue source to oil and timber extraction for these vulnerable peoples.

BAKING SODA

Outstanding leadership can even be found in products as humble as baking soda. It was members of two Canadian environmental groups who first knocked on Bryan Thomlison's door at Arm & Hammer, the baking soda company, to ask why the company was not educating consumers about baking soda's use as an alternative, non-toxic cleaner. Thirty-six months later, baking soda sales had risen 30 percent—in an industry in which sales had been stagnant for decades.

Thomlison began to deepen his relationships with other environmental stakeholders—environmental groups, educators, the media, regulators, and beyond. Further innovations followed. One of the founders of Earth Day USA asked if baking soda had ever been used to clean printed circuit boards, where traditional solvent cleaners were creating major CFC and VOC [volatile organic compound] problems. Thomlison put them in touch with the head of Research and Development. Two weeks later a prototype product was developed, which now forms the basis for a full line of patented industrial cleaners.

Arm & Hammer probably works more closely with environmental stakeholders than any other US company. We measured how much incremental value this stakeholder approach has created for the company, evaluating its contribution to new product development, revenues, and profit margins. While 15 percent of company revenues are derived from the "green" market, the company's stakeholder approach alone contributes an entirely incremental 5 percent of revenues. These incremental sales are created by the additional "green" consumers that this uniquely powerful stakeholder approach attracts. Furthermore, Arm & Hammer has found that its stakeholder strategy is twice as cost effective as traditional marketing approaches, generating $10 for every $1 invested, compared to $4 for the company's traditional marketing approach—yet another source of competitive advantage. . . .

THE BOTTOM LINE

Overall, the answer to the question, "Can it be profitable to conduct business in sustainable ways?" is certainly "Yes." Companies have gained competitive advantage by leveraging the environmental forces that are already reshaping and restructuring their marketplaces to create profitable business solutions to environmental challenges. This success often depends upon the quality of learning and innovation that these companies build into their relationships with environmental stakeholders. As a result of these companies' leadership, whole markets have continued to restructure towards more sustainable solutions.

By contrast, companies can choose to deny these new realities—and fail to introduce sustainable innovations. However, their businesses will continue to cause the environmental problems that fueled the market restructuring and ultimately create a downward, uncompetitive spiral. A profound lack of sustainability is certainly the hallmark of companies whose industries now face "dinosaur extinction" status. Decommissioning costs for the nuclear industry, for example, and even Superfund [a comprehensive Environmental Protection Agency program] clean-up costs for chemicals, place the long-term viability of both these industries in doubt unless ways can be found to pass the bill on to taxpayers.

The new paradigm may not, in fact, leave companies with much of a choice at all over the longer term. Interestingly, between 1979 and 1989, 47 percent of the "Fortune 500" organizations dropped off the "top 500" list there because they were not adaptive enough. As one commentator concluded: "*In the next decade, change or die.*" As the magnitude of the environmental challenges we face increases, sustainability will also increase in its effectiveness as a competitive strategy. Businesses may therefore find themselves saying over the next few decades: "*Sustain or die.*"

> "[The] profit-driven system is so all-pervasive that it is destroying the environment in every area of the world."

COMPANIES ARE FAILING TO PROTECT GLOBAL RESOURCES

Leonore Carpenter

Capitalism and unrestrained profitmaking are the driving force behind environmental destruction worldwide, Leonore Carpenter asserts in the following viewpoint. Carpenter maintains that under capitalism, companies are driven to produce large quantities of goods at the cheapest possible cost. This results in the use of inefficient production practices that waste resources and pollute the environment, according to Carpenter. To counteract the destructive effects of free-market business practices, Carpenter advocates the creation of a new union movement and an economic democracy that makes environmental protection its top priority. Carpenter is a pseudonym used by a writer for *New Unionist*, a monthly publication of the New Union political party.

As you read, consider the following questions:

1. What has international agribusiness done to peasants, according to Carpenter?
2. In the author's opinion, why have environmental laws failed?
3. According to Carpenter, what will the "next American Revolution" declare?

From Leonore Carpenter, "Profit vs. Earth," *New Unionist*, March 1995. Reprinted by permission of the New Union Party, Minneapolis, Minnesota.

It is to the advantage of the ruling powers of our modern world to promote the idea that environmental problems, as well as all the other problems facing us, are caused by "human nature." If the majority accepts this fatalistic view, all efforts for change are fruitless.

But a look at history shows that people's beliefs and feelings toward one another, and toward the environment, are conditioned by the society in which they live. And those beliefs and feelings change as society changes.

For thousands of years of tribal society, before the coming of civilization divided people into antagonistic classes, humans lived in basic harmony with each other and with their environment. Cooperation was the key to their survival and their advancement. Greed was unknown. The earth and its animals were worshiped as sacred beings. Even the necessary killing of game for food had to be justified through tribal rituals.

Although civilization took a mankind-centered attitude toward the environment, environmental destruction was at first incidental and occasional, until the period when capitalism, with its industrialization, became dominant. Also, the environmental damage of pre-capitalist societies was done in ignorance and had no overall long-term global impact.

THE CARNAGE CONTINUES

Today, while millions of dedicated individuals try to protect plant and animal life, and public opinion polls show that the majority is deeply concerned about the continuing destruction, the carnage continues. Why?

The presence of masses of people crowded into environmentally sensitive areas of the world creates the impression that overpopulation in itself is the main reason behind destruction of the environment. And without a doubt, there are too many people crowded into cities like Mexico City, and living in and near wilderness areas, which creates difficulties in many of the third world nations.

But overpopulation is a consequence of the workings out of capitalism, and is not the main reason for environmental stress.

For example, in vast areas of the third world, international agribusiness has thrown formerly self-reliant peasants off the best land in order to produce cash crops. Those who can't find work at poverty-level wages on the land they formerly owned have no choice but to migrate to cities where they hope to hire themselves out to industrial capitalists. Others are shoved out into the diminishing rain forests, which they try to make suitable for farming. These poor peasants are simply trying to survive and feed their families.

PROFIT-TAKING DESTROYS THE ENVIRONMENT

Profit, not the earth's survival, is what motivates international capitalist "investors." Directly or indirectly, the drive for profit affects everything around us and is the major reason for environmental destruction. This profit-driven system is so all-pervasive that it is destroying the environment in every area of the world. There is no land, no people, no species that has not been affected in one way or another.

In contrast to all previous social systems, the capitalist system is based on production for sale, and not for personal use or human welfare. Under capitalism, everything is a commodity to be bought and sold. Even labor is a commodity bought and sold on the labor market.

The capitalist system is governed by the laws of the market. There are essentially two "laws" of capitalism that dominate every business, large or small, and affect every decision made by companies.

The first is that every cost factor in production must be carefully weighed. Wages must be kept to a minimum. Raw materials must be bought at the lowest price, or replaced by cheaper substitutes. Waste must be disposed of as cheaply as possible, which leads to the indiscriminate and criminal dumping of toxic chemicals and other waste by-products of industry.

The second aspect of the market system which has a devastating effect on the environment is that the costs of production must be *constantly lowered*. Every new labor-saving invention installed by one company requires industry-wide imitation by its competitors. The result is that the total amount of commodities increases in astronomical proportions as the number of needed workers diminishes.

MORE AND MORE COMMODITIES

The need to sell ever-greater numbers of commodities creates, under capitalism, a throwaway culture. The system bombards us with commercials to buy, buy, buy, while creating products with a deliberately limited life span and which cost more to fix than replace. While it's good to have people recycle and consume fewer unneeded products, these personal choices alone can't redirect the underlying compulsions of the system that are the real reason for the environmental crisis.

While there is the need to sell ever-more commodities, the

working class has less purchasing power because companies are reducing their labor costs through layoffs and pay cuts. The corporations must then make greater efforts to sell in the international market.

But the corporations in each country face the same problem. Their respective working classes cannot buy back what they, the workers, create. With mounting inventories, the economic rivalry intensifies, and nothing is allowed to stand in the way of reducing costs to stay competitive. The rivalry leads ultimately to the greatest human and environmental disaster: war.

"IT'S THE SAME AGE-OLD QUESTION: IS THE LAKE HALF-POLLUTED, OR HALF-PRISTINE?"

© Kirk Anderson. Reprinted with permission.

Trying to solve environmental problems through government legislation has proved futile. Numerous laws that have been passed to protect the environment either are not enforced or are weakened in response to economic pressure from business. And the capitalists hold the ultimate weapon, the threat of moving their corporations to countries where there are no such laws.

It is economic power that gives the capitalist owning class, a tiny minority of less than 5% of the population, its tremendous political power. It logically follows that to redress our problems, we, the people, must gain economic power.

AN ECONOMIC DEMOCRACY

The foundation for a real democracy is the ownership and control of the economy by society as a whole—not by private corporations, not by the state, not by any other entity standing above us. To establish an economic democracy, we will need to organize in the workplaces to put ourselves in direct control of the economy, while at the same time organizing a political party to demand fundamental change.

We must build a new union movement based on the explicit goal of replacing capitalism with economic democracy. This new union movement will aim at organizing all of us, the entire working class, employed and unemployed, blue-collar and white-collar—all those who are today excluded from ownership of the means of production.

UNIONS UNITED AGAINST CAPITALISM

Through a system of elected and recallable representatives, unions on the local as well as national level would be united into one big union that would conduct a unified struggle against capitalism. While fighting the everyday battle between capital and labor, our union would always keep sight of its revolutionary goal, the democratic ownership and control of the industries, mandated by a majority vote for the workers' political party.

Once we have won this political victory, we, the producers, will build our new governing institutions based on the various industries. In addition to electing our immediate workplace management, we will send representatives to the local and national councils of our own particular industry, and to an all-industry Congress which will become the working government of the nation.

The change to an economic democracy will make it possible to solve the problems capitalism has created. With the absence of conflicting economic interests, the new society will be able to tackle problems in a spirit of cooperation. Our number-one priority will be conservation and protection of the environment, not only for ourselves, but to benefit future generations.

THE NEXT REVOLUTION

This is a call for a revolutionary transformation of society. The first American Revolution declared that the property of this country belongs to the people who inhabit it. The second American Revolution declared that the holding of human beings as property is immoral and illegal. The next American Revolution will declare that the means of life, the industries, rightfully belong to all the people.

This will not be a simple or easy process. We workers need to rediscover the common needs and hopes that bind us as a class, that override our differences and diversity. In this dog-eat-dog world, we must realize that the unemployed and homeless are victims of the same system that exploits workers with jobs.

Above all, we need to understand that we, the working class, are the only necessary class. We do all the world's useful work, and we are the only ones who can change it for the better.

PERIODICAL BIBLIOGRAPHY

The following articles have been selected to supplement the diverse views presented in this chapter. Addresses are provided for periodicals not indexed in the *Readers' Guide to Periodical Literature*, the *Alternative Press Index*, the *Social Sciences Index*, or the *Index to Legal Periodicals and Books*.

Business and Society Review	Special section on private sector efforts to protect global resources, Summer 1994. Available from Management Reports Inc., PO Box 603, Westport, CT 06880.
Eileen B. Claussen	"U.S. and Business: Partners in Addressing Global Environmental Issues," *U.S. Department of State Dispatch*, July 8, 1996.
CQ Researcher	Special issue on property rights, June 16, 1995. Available from Congressional Quarterly, 1414 22nd St. NW, Washington, DC 20037.
Terrence Heath	"A Vicious Circle," *UNESCO Courier*, September 1996.
Udi Helman	"Sustainable Development: Strategies for Reconciling Environment and Economy in the Developing World," *Washington Quarterly*, Fall 1995. Available from MIT Press, 55 Hayward St., Cambridge, MA 02142.
Daniel J. Kevles	"Endangered Environmentalists," *New York Review of Books*, February 20, 1997.
Joseph T. Ling	"Design for Sustainability," *Vital Speeches of the Day*, January 1, 1996.
Richard A. Matthew	"The Greening of U.S. Foreign Policy," *Issues in Science and Technology*, Fall 1996.
Brigid McMenamin	"Environmental Imperialism," *Forbes*, May 20, 1996.
Don Stap	"Returning the Natives," *Audubon*, November/December 1996.
David Vogel	"Reconciling Free Trade with Responsible Regulation," *Issues in Science and Technology*, Fall 1995.

FOR FURTHER DISCUSSION

CHAPTER 1

1. L.F. Ivanhoe maintains that global oil reserves are being exhausted. The American Petroleum Institute and John L. Kennedy counter that the global oil supply is abundant. How might one go about further investigation to determine which viewpoint is more valid?

2. What does Dennis T. Avery mean by the term "doomsayers"? Does this word have positive or negative connotations? Does his use of this word strengthen or weaken his argument? Explain your answer.

3. According to the president of Guatemala, cited by Arthur Golden and Matt Miller, "If we fail to preserve the rain forests, more people will die than have perished in world wars." Do you believe that this statement is credible? Why or why not? How do you think Michael Sanera and Jane S. Shaw would respond to this remark?

CHAPTER 2

1. Organic farmers avoid the use of chemicals and pesticides to grow food. Dennis T. Avery contends that the use of these products helps produce higher food yields. Do you believe that it is more important to reduce the use of chemicals or to increase food yields? Explain your reasoning.

2. Richard Schwartz uses statistics to argue that livestock agriculture production consumes tremendous amounts of resources, causes deforestation, and fouls the environment. The National Cattlemen's Beef Association cites statistics to show that there is no relationship between livestock grazing and deforestation and that beef production uses water and energy efficiently. Did either author's use of statistics sway your opinion? Which author uses statistics to a greater advantage?

3. Susanne L. Huttner contends that genetically engineered foods should be produced. John B. Fagan maintains that the consumption of such foods could harm the human body. After considering both authors' evidence, would you knowingly eat foods that were genetically engineered? Why or why not?

CHAPTER 3

1. Christopher Flavin is an associate project director for the Worldwatch Institute, a staunch advocate of renewable energy. Bertram Wolfe is a former nuclear industry manager. How are the backgrounds of these two authors evident in their views about energy? What does Wolfe say about the hope of finding a "new, clean, plentiful energy source"? How do you think Flavin would respond to Wolfe's statement? Explain your answer.

2. Rémi Tremblay argues that dependence on gasoline and automobiles for transportation is damaging land, the atmosphere, and human health. Lee R. Raymond asserts that the petroleum industry is spending billions of dollars annually on environmental improvement. Which author makes a stronger case? Support your answer with examples from the viewpoints.

3. The authors in this chapter advocate the use of a variety of energy sources. After considering their cost and environmental impact, rank these sources according to their suitability for society.

CHAPTER 4

1. Earnie Deavenport argues that free-market activities such as technological innovation and economic growth reduce environmental harm. Jerry Mander contends that an unrestricted free market and increasing consumption is destroying agricultural land and habitats. After reading both viewpoints, whose argument do you find more reliable? Why? Which of the viewpoints comes closer to what you believed before reading them?

2. Sue Hall maintains that the incentive of increased profits is driving companies to act in a more sustainable manner. What examples does she use to support her argument? Does Leonore Carpenter's viewpoint effectively refute Hall's examples? Why or why not?

ORGANIZATIONS TO CONTACT

The editors have compiled the following list of organizations concerned with the issues debated in this book. The descriptions are derived from materials provided by the organizations. All have publications or information available for interested readers. The list was compiled on the date of publication of the present volume; names, addresses, phone and fax numbers, and e-mail and Internet addresses may change. Be aware that many organizations take several weeks or longer to respond to inquiries, so allow as much time as possible.

Chemical Manufacturers Association (CMA)
1300 Wilson Blvd., Arlington, VA 22209
(703) 741-5000 • fax: (703) 741-6000

The CMA is a national association of chemical companies. It conducts technical research and monitors legislation and regulations regarding environmental safety and health. The association also provides the public with health and safety information about chemicals. In addition to numerous booklets, its publications include the magazine ChemEcology and the newsletter CMA News, each published ten times a year.

Competitive Enterprise Institute (CEI)
1001 Connecticut Ave. NW, Suite 1250, Washington, DC 20036
(202) 331-1010 • fax: (202) 331-0640
e-mail: info@cei.org • Internet: http://www.cei.org

The CEI encourages the use of the free market and private property rights to protect the environment. It advocates removing governmental regulatory barriers and establishing a system in which the private sector would be responsible for the environment. CEI's publications include the monthly newsletter CEI Update, the book The True State of the Planet, and the monograph "Federal Agriculture Policy: A Harvest of Environmental Abuse."

Earth Island Institute
300 Broadway, Suite 28, San Francisco, CA 94133
(415) 788-3666 • fax: (415) 788-7324
e-mail: earthisland@earthisland.org
Internet: http://www.earthisland.org

Earth Island Institute's work addresses environmental issues and their relation to such concerns as human rights and economic development in the Third World. The institute's publications include the quarterly Earth Island Journal.

Environmental Defense Fund (EDF)
257 Park Ave. South, New York, NY 10010
(212) 505-2100 • fax: (212) 505-0892
Internet: http://www.edf.org

The fund is a public interest organization of lawyers, scientists, and economists dedicated to the protection and improvement of environmental quality and public health. It publishes the bimonthly *EDF Letter* and the report "Plastics Recycling: How Slow Can It Grow?"

Friends of the Earth
1025 Vermont Ave. NW, Suite 300, Washington, DC 20005
(202) 783-7400

Friends of the Earth is dedicated to protecting the planet from environmental disaster and to preserving biological diversity. The organization encourages toxic waste cleanup and promotes the use of tax dollars to protect the environment. Its publications include the bimonthly newsletter *Friends of the Earth* and the books *Crude Awakening, the Oil Mess in America: Wasting Energy, Jobs, and the Environment* and *Earth Budget: Making Our Tax Dollars Work for the Environment.*

Greenpeace U.S.A.
1436 U St. NW, Washington, DC 20009
(202) 462-1177 • fax: (202) 462-4507
e-mail: greenpeace@wdc.greenpeace.org
Internet: http://www.greenpeace.org/usa

Greenpeace opposes nuclear energy and the use of toxic chemicals and supports ocean and wildlife preservation. It uses controversial direct-action techniques and strives for media coverage of its actions in an effort to educate the public. It publishes the quarterly magazine *Greenpeace* and the books *Radiation and Health, Coastline,* and *The Greenpeace Book on Antarctica.*

The Heritage Foundation
214 Massachusetts Ave. NE, Washington, DC 20002
(202) 546-4400 • fax: (202) 546-0904

The Heritage Foundation is a conservative think tank that supports the principles of free enterprise and limited government in environmental matters. Its many publications include the quarterly magazine *Policy Review* and the occasional papers series Heritage Talking Points, which periodically includes studies on environmental regulations and government policies.

Hudson Institute
Herman Kahn Center
5395 Emerson Way, PO Box 26-919, Indianapolis, IN 46226
(317) 545-1000 • fax: (317) 545-1384
e-mail: johnmc@hii.hudson.org • Internet: http://www.hudson.org

The Hudson Institute is a public policy research center whose members are elected from academia, government, and industry. The institute promotes the power of the free market and human ingenuity to solve environmental problems. Its publications include the monthly *Outlook* and the monthly policy bulletin *Foresight.*

Natural Resources Defense Council (NRDC)

40 W. 20th St., New York, NY 10011
(212) 727-2700 • fax: (212) 727-1773
Internet: http://www.nrdc.org

The council is an environmental group composed of lawyers and scientists who conduct litigation and research on toxic waste and other environmental hazards. The NRDC publishes pamphlets, brochures, reports, books, and the quarterly *Amicus Journal*.

Political Economy Research Center (PERC)

502 S. 19th Ave., Suite 211, Bozeman, MT 59715
(406) 587-9591
Internet: http://www.perc.org

PERC is a research and education foundation that focuses primarily on environmental and natural resource issues. It emphasizes the advantages of free markets and the importance of private property rights in environmental protection. PERC's publications include the quarterly newsletter *PERC Reports* and papers in the *PERC Policy Series*.

Rainforest Action Network (RAN)

450 Sansome St., Suite 700, San Francisco, CA 94111
(415) 398-2732 • fax: (415) 398-2732
e-mail: rainforest@ran.org • Internet: http://www.ran.org

RAN works to preserve the world's rain forests through activism and education addressing the logging and importing of tropical timber, cattle ranching in rain forests, and the rights of indigenous rain forest peoples. RAN's publications include the monthly bulletin *Action Report* and the semiannual *World Rainforest Report*.

Reason Foundation

3415 S. Sepulveda Blvd., Suite 400, Los Angeles, CA 90034-6064
(310) 391-2245 • fax: (310) 391-4395

The Reason Foundation is a libertarian public policy research organization. Its environmental research focuses on issues such as energy, global warming, and recycling. The foundation publishes the monthly magazine *Reason* and the books *Global Warming: The Greenhouse, White House, and Poor House Effect*, *The Case Against Electric Vehicle Mandates in California*, and *Solid Waste Recycling Costs—Issues and Answers*.

Stockholm Environment Institute (SEI)

11 Arlington St., Boston, MA 02116-3411
(617) 266-8090 • fax: (617) 266-8303
e-mail: praskin@tellus.com
Internet: http://www.channel1.com/users/tellus/seib.html

Headquartered in Sweden, the SEI is an internationally networked research institute that focuses on a variety of environmental issues, including climate change, energy use, and freshwater resources. The SEI publishes *SEI: An International Environment Bulletin* four times a year, the *Energy Report* twice a year, and *Environmental Perspectives* three times a year.

World Bank (IBRD)
Environment Department, 1818 H St. NW, Washington, DC 20433
(202) 477-1234 • fax: (202) 577-0565
Internet: http://www.worldbank.org

Formally known as the International Bank for Reconstruction and Development (IBRD), the World Bank seeks to reduce poverty and improve the standards of living of poor people around the world. It promotes sustainable growth and investments in developing countries through loans, technical assistance, and policy guidance. Many of the Bank's projects focus on agriculture, biodiversity, and energy. Its Environment Department publishes the periodicals *Environment Bulletin, Annual Report on the Environment,* and *Facing the Global Environment Change;* several series, including the Social Assessment Series and the Climate Change Series; and individual publications on environmental progress and desertification.

World Resources Institute (WRI)
1709 New York Ave. NW, Washington, DC 20006
(202) 638-6300 • fax: (202) 638-0036

The WRI conducts research on global resources and environmental conditions. It holds briefings, seminars, and conferences and provides the print and broadcast media with new perspectives and background materials on environmental issues. The institute publishes reports, papers, and the books *The Right Climate for Carbon Taxes: Creating Economic Incentives to Protect the Atmosphere* and *How We Can Slow Global Warming.*

Worldwatch Institute
1776 Massachusetts Ave. NW, Washington, DC 20036-1904
(202) 452-1999 • fax: (202) 296-7365

Worldwatch is a research organization that analyzes and calls attention to global problems, including environmental concerns such as the loss of cropland, forests, habitat, species, and water supplies. It compiles the annual *State of the World* anthology and publishes the bimonthly magazine *World Watch* and the Worldwatch Paper Series, which includes "Clearing the Air: A Global Agenda" and "The Climate of Hope: New Strategies for Stabilizing the World's Atmosphere."

BIBLIOGRAPHY OF BOOKS

Tom Athanasiou — Divided Planet: The Ecology of Rich and Poor. Boston: Little, Brown, 1996.

Ronald Bailey, ed. — Eco-Scam: The False Prophets of Ecological Apocalypse. New York: St. Martin's Press, 1993.

Ronald Bailey, ed. — The True State of the Planet. New York: Free Press, 1995.

Edward B. Barbier, Joanne C. Burgess, and Carl Folke — Paradise Lost? The Ecological Economics of Biodiversity. London: Earthscan, 1994.

Jeremy Brecher and Tim Costello — World Disorder: Global Village or Global Pillage. Boston: South End Press, 1994.

David Ross Brower with Steve Chappel — Let the Mountains Talk, the Rivers Run: A Call to Those Who Would Save the Earth. San Francisco: HarperCollins West, 1995.

Alston Chase — In a Dark Wood: The Fight over Forests and the Rising Tyranny of Ecology. Boston: Houghton Mifflin, 1995.

Patrick Clawson — The Ends of the Earth: A Journey at the Dawn of the Twenty-first Century. New York: Random House, 1996.

Theo Colburn, Dianne Dumanoski, and John Peterson Myers — Our Stolen Future: Are We Threatening Our Fertility, Intelligence, and Survival? A Scientific Detective Story. New York: Dutton, 1996.

James R. Dunn and John E. Kinney — Conservative Environmentalism: Reassessing the Means, Redefining the Ends. Westport, CT: Quorum Publishing, 1996.

Gregg Easterbrook — A Moment on the Earth: The Coming of Age of Environmental Optimism. New York: Viking, 1995.

Paul R. Ehrlich, Anne H. Ehrlich, and Gretchen C. Daily — The Stork and the Plow: The Equity Answer to the Human Dilemma. New York: Putnam, 1995.

Michael Fumento — Science Under Siege: Balancing Technology and the Environment. New York: William Morrow, 1993.

Robert O. Keohane and Marc A. Levy, eds. — Institutions for Environmental Aid: Pitfalls and Promise. Cambridge, MA: MIT Press, 1996.

John Kirby, Phil O'Keefe, and Lloyd Timberlake, eds. — The Earthscan Reader in Sustainable Development. London: Earthscan, 1996.

John Lemons and Donald A. Brown, eds. — Sustainable Development: Science, Ethics, and Public Policy. Boston: Kluwer Academic Publishers, 1995.

Jerry Mander and Edward Goldsmith — The Case Against the Global Economy and for a Turn to the Local. San Francisco: Sierra Club Books, 1996.

Donella H. Meadows et al.	*Beyond the Limits: Confronting Global Collapse, Envisioning a Sustainable Future.* Post Mills, VT: Chelsea Green, 1992.
Roger E. Meiners and Bruce Yandle, eds.	*Taking the Environment Seriously.* Lanham, MD: Rowman & Littlefield, 1995.
Patrick J. Michaels	*Sound and Fury: The Science and Politics of Global Warming.* Washington, DC: Cato Institute, 1993.
Norman Myers and Julian Simon	*Scarcity or Abundance? A Debate on the Environment.* New York: Norton, 1994.
John O'Conner, ed.	*Monitoring Environmental Progress.* Washington, DC: World Bank, 1995.
David Pearce and Dominic Moran	*The Economic Value of Biodiversity.* London: Earthscan, 1994.
Jane A. Peterson, ed.	*Partnership for the Planet: An Environmental Agenda for the United Nations.* Washington, DC: Worldwatch Institute, 1995.
Gareth Porter and Janet Welsh Brown	*Global Environmental Politics.* Boulder, CO: Westview Press, 1996.
Michael Power	*Environmental Protection and Economic Well-Being: The Economic Pursuit of Quality.* Armonk, NY: M.E. Sharpe, 1996.
Shridath Ramphal	*Our Country, the Planet: Forging a Partnership for Survival.* Washington, DC: Island Press, 1992.
Dixy Lee Ray and Lou Guzzo	*Environmental Overkill: Whatever Happened to Common Sense?* Washington, DC: Regnery Gateway, 1993.
Bruce Rich	*Mortgaging the Earth: The World Bank, Environmental Impoverishment, and the Crisis of Development.* Boston: Beacon Press, 1994.
Julian Simon, ed.	*The State of Humanity.* Cambridge, MA: Blackwell, 1995.
Y. Suzuki, K. Ueta, and S. Mori	*Global Environmental Security: From Protection to Prevention.* New York: Springer-Verlag, 1996.
Paul B. Thompson	*The Spirit of the Soil: Agriculture and Environmmental Ethics.* New York: Routledge Press, 1995.
John Vandemeer and Ivette Perfecto	*Breakfast of Biodiversity: The Truth About Rain Forest Destruction.* Oakland, CA: Food First Books, 1995.
Aaron Wildavsky	*But Is It True? A Citizen's Guide to Environmental Health and Safety Issues.* Cambridge, MA: Harvard University Press, 1995.

INDEX

Advanced Boiling Water Reactor, 120
Advanced Liquid Metal Reactor, 116
Africa
  state of rain forests in, 49
The Age of Missing Information (McKibben), 134
agriculture
  biotechnological potentials of, 85
  livestock
    is wasteful of resources, 75
    should be abolished, 75
    utilizes resources that would be wasted, 81, 82
    waste management in, 80–81
  organic
    cost of, 67
    definition of, 65
    is unsustainable, 70, 72
    sale of products, 66
alternative fuels, 24
American Petroleum Institute, 25
aquifers
  depletion of, 35
Arco, 167
Arctic National Wildlife Refuge, 27
Arm & Hammer, 168, 169
automobile industry
  link with oil industry, 126–27, 130, 137
  resistance to electric vehicles by, 126
automobiles
  are major pollutants, 129
  electric vehicles are efficient alternative to, 123
  real cost of owning and operating, 130
Avery, Dennis T., 39, 69, 81

Babbitt, Bruce, 119
Bailey, Ronald, 151
baking soda
  replacement of toxic cleaners by, 168–69
Basel Convention, 153
Begley, Ed, Jr., 123
biotechnology
  effects in developing world, 161
  federal oversight of, 87–88
  is minimal, 92
  is threat to food supply, 95–96
  will increase crop yields, 44
BP Statistical Review of World Energy, 21
Brown, Lester R., 32, 40, 43, 44
By Bread Alone (Brown), 40

Callejas, Rafael Leonardo, 53

capitalism
  is destroying environment, 173
  should be replaced by economic democracy, 174–75
Carpenter, Leonore, 171
Carpio, Ramiro de León, 50
carryover stocks, 33, 34
  as indicator of food security, 35
  low levels of, 40–41
Chernobyl reactor, 117
Chiapas (Mexico), 50
China
  increase in grain imports by, 33, 41
  overuse of aquifers in, 35
climate change, 116
  deforestation contributes to, 48
  farmers will have to cope with, 33
  fossil fuels contribute to, 116
  is linked to global economic expansion, 159
Conservation Resource Program, 37
Consumers Union, 88
CQ Researcher, 86
cropland
  is underutilized, 44
  unsustainable use of, 35
crop yields
  biotechnology will increase, 44
  organic farmers need breakthrough in, 71–72

Deavenport, Earnie, 148
debt-for-nature swaps, 57–58
deforestation
  causes of, 50
  in Central America, 51
  contributes to climate change, 48
  extent of has been exaggerated, 54
  has reached crisis proportions, 47
  link with new diseases, 160–61
  livestock grazing has not contributed to, 81–82
  in Malaysia, 51, 52–53
  in Philippines, 52
developing world
  economic growth will ease problems of, 141
  effects of agribusiness in, 172–73
  farm output is growing in, 41
  population growth is falling in, 42–43
    con, 116
  prospects for wind power in, 112–13
  solar technologies for, 106–107
The Development Dictionary (Sachs), 159
dish-stirling generators, 106

forestalls oil exhaustion, 27
is increasing oil reserves, 139
Philippines
deforestation in, 52
photovoltaic technology
efficiency levels of, 103
is ideal for small installations, 107
Plataforma Solar de Almeria, 105
population
of developing world
is falling, 42–43
will double in 21st century, 116
is encroaching on rain forests, 49
is stabilizing, 42
The Population Bomb (Ehrlich), 45
Power Surge (Flavin and Lenssen), 112
President's Council on Sustainable
Development, 152

rain forests
are harmed by globalization, 161
data on, 56
maximizing land-use efficiency will
save, 45
population is encroaching on, 49
positive developments for, 57
prescription drugs from, 59
see also deforestation
Raymond, Lee R., 136
Recombinant DNA technology, 85, 86
Russell, Dick, 123
Russia, oil production in
barriers to, 28

Sachs, Wolfgang, 159
San Diego Union-Tribune, 47
Sanera, Michael, 54
Saving the Planet with Pesticides and Plastic
(Avery), 81
Schwartz, Richard, 75
Shaman Pharmaceuticals, 164, 168
Shaw, Jane S., 54
Simon, Julian L., 28, 43
Singer, Fred S., 119
solar energy
vs. fossil fuels, 101–102
storage problem of, 104
use should be increased, 100
solar power stations, 105
decentralized units, 106–107
State of the World: 1996 (Brown), 44

Technology Review, 125
Third World. *See* developing world
Three Mile Island, 118
Tremblay, Rémi, 128

The True State of the Planet (Bailey), 151

The Ultimate Resource (Simon), 28
UN Food and Agriculture Organization,
45
on rain forest clearance, 56
up-draft power stations, 106
U.S. Food and Drug Administration, 87
U.S. Geological Survey
estimate on world oil production, 26

vegetarianism
health benefits of are unproven, 83
is important for global survival, 78
vehicles
electric
are an efficient alternative to gas-
powered cars, 123
battery technology and, 126
development of, 131
human-powered, advantages of,
132–34

Wall Street Journal, 43
Ward, Barbara, 149
Ward Valley (California) Repository,
119
Washington Times, 119
water resources
consumption for livestock
production, 77
is minimal, 83
for urban vs. agricultural use,
competition for, 37–38
Wellman (chemical company), 164
wildlands
are not being lost to population
growth, 45
see also rain forests
wind power
in Europe, 111
generation capacity of, 110
potential of, 113–14
roots of, 109–11
in U.S., 112
Wolfe, Bertram, 115
Woodruff, David, 48
World & I (periodical), 104
World Resources Institute, 130
World Trade Organization (WTO),
156–57
Worldwatch Paper, 131

Yucca Mountain (Nevada), 118,
119–20

zero-energy house, 102-103

DATE DUE

Demco, Inc. 38-293